Hubert Smith
Long Close
North Chideock.

THE CHURCHES OF DEVON

By the same author

Dicky Slader, the Exmoor Pedlar Poet
Days of Renown
Downalong the Exe

North Molton: c 1450. A fine church enriched by the late medieval mining industry

The Churches of Devon

by

J. M. SLADER

DAVID & CHARLES : NEWTON ABBOT

7153 4255 X

To the Clergy and People of Devon

Printed in Great Britain by
W J Holman Limited Dawlish
for David & Charles (Holdings) Limited
South Devon House Newton Abbot Devon

CONTENTS

LIST OF ILLUSTRATIONS

PLANS AND MAPS

Preface

The idea for this book was conceived in my father's library at Tavistock before the last war. It was during this period of my youth that I first became interested in the parish churches of Devon, which often stood near to the Wesleyan chapels where my father preached. Except for East Anglia, these Devon churches, with their neighbours in Somerset, are among the finest in Britain. Much has been written about them and their contents, but the information is widely scattered over many volumes and no one has yet attempted a survey covering the whole thousand years. What I have tried to do is to present their story, without bias towards any particular period, in the form of a comprehensive survey. Complete it can never be, for churches will continue to be built as long as mankind cares for his spiritual well-being. Their plan, or their use, may change, as after the Reformation, but whatever form they take they will remain buildings of interest. The churches of England are part of our precious heritage and unique among the nations of the world.

I am indebted to earlier authors whose writings have influenced me during the compiling of this volume, above all to Professor Nikolaus Pevsner whose work in 'The Buildings of England' series (*North Devon* and *South Devon*, Penguin Books Ltd) is of great value to ecclesiologists. My thanks are also offered to many people, too numerous to list individually, including both clergy and laity, who have greatly assisted me. I would like specially to thank my wife, without whose patience, understanding and assistance this book could not have been written. My grateful acknowledgements also go to the Editor of the *Western Morning News* for permission to reproduce information from articles of mine which have appeared in that newspaper.

Finally, three notes of explanation: North Petherwin and Werrington were transferred to the County of Cornwall on 1 April 1966 and their churches are not, therefore, included in this survey. Also excluded is any detailed account of Devon church bells, since a survey of these would require a volume to itself. Similarly, a survey of Exeter Cathedral on a scale adequate to the theme has yet to be written, and the Cathedral, therefore, is mentioned in this book only where its construction bears some relation to the churches of the county.

J M SLADER

Abergavenny
March, 1968

Note : Since writing this book St Michael, Torquay, has been demolished to make way for a supermarket

I. Ten Devon Churches of Outstanding Interest

BRANSCOMBE

One of the most beautiful coastal parishes in England, Branscombe has altered little since W. H. Hudson, gathering impressions for his book *Afoot in England*, came this way sixty years ago. Its church, essentially of Norman origin, represents a thousand years of ecclesiastical history. On the outbreak of the second world war, 700 detailed photographs of it were taken as a precaution against its destruction, so that it is probably the best documented church in England.

Branscombe: dedicated to St Winifred,
a Welsh missionary who possibly preached here, *c* 650

CREDITON

A medieval town church of exceptional interest, whose history began with the birth of the great missionary Winifred, or St Boniface, the apostle of Central Germany who was martyred in 756. From 910 AD to 1050 AD it was the seat of the bishop. Well restored and notable for work of the Decorated period, it contains some fine nineteenth-century glass and some interesting modern fittings. It is also one of the very few Devon churches with a clerestory.

Crediton: the memorial over the west wall of the tower is by Caroë, to General Sir Redvers Buller, KCB, VC

CULLOMPTON

Few valleys in England can offer such medieval ecclesiastical splendour as this fine example of the Perpendicular. It is the cloth industry's thanksgiving for its prosperity and an enduring memorial to John Lane, a merchant, and others like Roger Stockman, clerk, who in 1545 left 'so moche to the new tower as will paye for a foot square'.

Cullompton: its impressive list of vicars dates back to 1181

EXETER, ST DAVID

The third church to have stood on this site, and the finest example of Victorian ecclesiastical architecture west of Bristol. With its lofty arches, wide roof span and spaciousness, it conveys an immediate impression of simple dignity and, with the passing of years, has assumed its rightful place in a city which looks back over 2,000 years of history.

Exeter, St David: built 1897-1900, with an imaginative north-east tower and typical Victorian interior

HARTLAND

Often called 'The Cathedral of North Devon', Hartland church is noteworthy for its roofs, the wide span of its nave arches from the Decorated period, and its early Perpendicular tower and roodscreen. Its long history began with the preaching of a Christian missionary, Nectan, to whom the church is dedicated.

Hartland: for nearly 500 years the tower has stood as a landmark on land and at sea

MILBER, NEWTON ABBOT

Modern yet not modernistic, Milber church represents a new and original departure in church planning and may justly claim to be the most exciting church built in Devon since the Reforma- tion. The workmanship of the interior is excellent and the fittings are admirably in keeping with the design and conception.

Milber, Newton Abbot: sometimes known as 'The Dream Church',
its plan is based upon that revealed in a dream of the Reverend W. Keble Martin

MOLLAND

A typical Devon village church of the eighteenth century, happily 'unrestored' by the Victorians—rustic, plastered and whitewashed throughout. The box pews, canopied three-decker pulpit, leaning piers and plastered tympanum completely filling the chancel opening are characteristically Georgian. Until 1915 it was held in plurality with Knowstone and its vicars included the notorious John Froude.

Molland: often overlooked are the medieval bells one of which, dated 1562, is among the oldest dated bells in England

OTTERY ST MARY

English Gothic in all its splendour—with nave and chancel of equal length, and Early English transepts—the church of Ottery St Mary is renowned throughout the West of England. The majestic austerity of the design, stately yet dignified, is surpassed by few other churches of similar size. The Victorian restoration was the work of William Butterfield, builder of Balliol and Keble Colleges.

Ottery St Mary: like Crediton, a Collegiate Church.
The entire fabric has been restored since the second world war

TEIGNGRACE

A departure from tradition in a traditional county and architecturally interesting as an early example of Strawberry Hill Gothic. One of the many 'family' village churches in Devon, Teigngrace is indebted to the eighteenth-century Templer family for their courage in creating so 'modernistic' an interior, which today enjoys a beauty and serenity seldom found.

Teigngrace: the monuments to the Templer family are of interest and, with one exception, they are unsigned

TORBRYAN

A typical Devon village church of the era of fine tracery in stone and craftsmanship in wood. Completely characteristic in plan and fittings, it represents, with the nearby Church House Inn, the village social life of medieval England, when the church building was at once a theatre, an assembly hall and a place of worship.

Torbryan: the exterior is notable for its Devon tower, two-storeyed porch and fine Perpendicular windows

2. Pre-Conquest

As is the case with so many Cornish churches, the earliest churches of Devon owe their origins to the journeyings of the Celtic saints who came from Ireland and Wales during the sixth and seventh centuries. These holy men are known to have landed within the confines of Barnstaple Bay—a natural point of entry—and several sites in the area are still associated with the Christianity they came to

Landkey, late fifteenth century: it was here that St Kea preached nearly a thousand years earlier

preach. Notable among them are those now occupied by the churches of:

St Helen	-	Abbotsham and Lundy
St Brannoc	-	Braunton
St Fili	-	Filleigh
St Nectan	-	Hartland and Welcombe
St John	-	Instow
St Kea	-	Landkey
St Petrock	-	Parracombe

Among these missionaries was St Petrock, perhaps the most successful of all, and the Celtic saints, Indract and Dominic, who landed in the closing years of the seventh century at a port called 'Tamerunta', which can only have been Tamerton Foliot. St Budoc, too, landed in the same creek and founded a church at Budshead (now in St Budeaux). Branscombe is dedicated to an obscure Welsh saint, St Winnifred, *c* 650, and another Celtic saint, Rumon, gave his name to Romansleigh where, close by the church dedicated to him, are the scanty remains of his holy well. Marystow, which means 'the holy place of St Mary', could point to a pre-Conquest church, as could Ugborough where the church and churchyard are entirely contained within a small earthwork of Saxon date. Other indications of the presence of churches in very early times are afforded by the village names of Hawkchurch, meaning 'Hafoc's church' and Whitchurch, 'white church', which was probably built of the white elvan found on Roborough Down.

Devon was incorporated in the see of Sherborne in AD 705 and though a minster had been founded at Crediton in 739—King Ethelheard granted twenty hides of land for the founding of a monastery 'in a place called Creedy'—the see of Crediton was not created until 909, and did not move to Exeter until 1050. Other early minsters existed at Axminster, where Cynehard, an Anglo-Saxon prince, was brought for burial in 786; at Exminster, an ancient village dating from the first days of the Saxon occupation, and at Plympton and Coryton. In the year 857, Brannocmynster, as the settlement was then called, was given to Glastonbury Abbey 'for the taking of salmon' and in the following century Bishop Ethelgar (934-53) collected funds for the building of St Mary's Minster at Crediton. Tradition has it that the foundations of this vanished Saxon cathedral lie beneath the present churchyard, and during the restoration of the lady chapel between 1876 and 1877 some ancient masonry laid bare did indeed suggest an archway leading to a crypt, but unfortunately no further investigation was made.

The missal of Leofric, the last Saxon bishop, indicates that there was a church at 'Oc mund tune' (Okehampton) during his lifetime. It occupied the same site as the present church and, clustered about it, was the Saxon village which Baldwin de Brionne, the Norman sheriff of Devon, abandoned when he built Okehampton town between the East Okement and West Okement rivers. Leofric also describes the original foundation by St Curig in 561 of the church at Coryton (*vid,* Curigs Town), which was re-dedicated in 1261 by Bishop Bronescombe to St Andrew. At Paignton, there was a church on the present site as far back as the tenth century and water-worn foundation stones of that period are said to lie beneath the present floor. At Colyton, the Saxon cross to be seen in the south transept gives some idea of the antiquity of the village. The stone in the south porch of Lustleigh church inscribed 'DETREID OC CON HINOC' is probably a ninth-century tombstone. A pre-Conquest building dedicated to St Petrock is also said to have existed at Lewtrenchard. It was rebuilt in 1261 and re-dedicated to St Peter.

In the mid-tenth century the county boasted four burhs—Exeter, Lydford, Pilton and Totnes—and at each of these in 1018 we hear of a burhwitan, a form of 'borough council', capable of taking note of official transactions. As market towns, these burhs would have had their own churches and minted their own coins. At Lydford, excavations have proved the existence of an early oratory, and we know there was a church at Pilton attached to a Benedictine priory—a cell to the abbey of Malmesbury—which, according to Leland, was founded by Athelstan (925-40). At Branscombe the church was probably built, or rebuilt, about 925, the year when Athelstan gave Branscombe, with other estates, to the Benedictine house of St Peter at Exeter.

East Teignmouth, whose present church is entirely Victorian, is mentioned in a Saxon charter of 1044. The structure would seem to have been of the 'nave tower' type, characteristic of the period, in which the base of the tower formed the body of the church. The tower had a fortress-like appearance, rising immediately from the ground with a circular stair-turret at the south-west angle in three diminishing stages, ending at the summit in a conical cap. East of the tower stood a small chancel and a small nave structure with a south porch immediately west of it, both very much narrower than the tower.

Prof W. G. Hoskins (*Devon*, 1954) inclines to the belief that all, or nearly all, the true nucleated villages possessed a church by the eleventh century.

Oak being abundantly available in the interior, the earliest churches were built mostly of timber, wattle and clay, but with stone foundations, much in the manner of the remarkable Saxon church still standing at Greenstead in Essex. Later, stone became the chief material, as in the early Saxon church at East Teignmouth.

At Sidbury, the small and completely plain crypt (9 ft by 10 ft) beneath the western part of the chancel is generally accepted as being of an earlier date than the twelfth-century work immediately above it. Supporting evidence of this is provided not only by the different character of the masonry,

but also by the fact that the upper walls are built only in part upon the lower, as the axis of the chancel differs from that of the crypt. The nave pillars are set upon the walls of the earlier Saxon church, which were cut down to a height of only four feet to serve as foundations. The Sidbury crypt is one of the only six Saxon crypts in England.

Some 120 Devon churches were under the administration of Bishop Osbern (1073), according to the Domesday survey made in the middle of his episcopate. Even at this early date, the Church held considerable property in the county, estimated at one-seventh of the cultivated area or one-fifth of

Braunton. Mostly thirteenth century: St Brannoc is buried beneath the high altar

the assessed value of the whole. The following is a list of churches, and chapels which were at that time dependent upon a 'mother church', nearly all of which are today represented by parish churches:

1. Exeter Cathedral and sixteen dependent churches: St Martin's, Exeter (consecrated 1065); St Sidwell's, Exeter; Ashburton, Branscombe, Clyst Honiton, Colebrooke, Culmstock, Dawlish, East Teignmouth, Ide, Salcombe Regis, Sidbury, St Marychurch, Staverton, Stoke Canon, Topsham.
2. St Stephen's, Exeter; and seven others, all belonging to the Bishop: Chudleigh, Morchard Bishop, Paignton, Stoke Gabriel, Swimbridge, Bishops Nympton, Bishops Tawton.
3. St Olave's, Exeter; and one dependent church—Sherford.
4. Ten Prebendal churches with eight dependents: St Mary's in the castle of Exeter, Axminster, Braunton, Cullompton, Crediton, Hartland, Newton Ferrers, Plympton (also a priory church)—with chapels of Dean Prior, Egg Buckland, Maristowe, Sampford Spinney, Shaugh Prior, Thrushelton and Wembury; South Molton, Totnes—with St Peter's chapel.

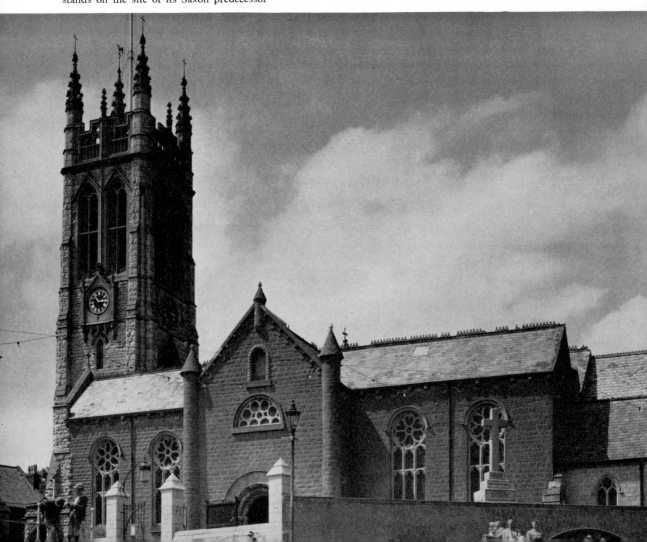

East Teignmouth. Wholly Victorian, though it stands on the site of its Saxon predecessor

5. Seven parochial churches or chapels: Barnstaple, Colyton, Exminster, Kingskerswell, Pinhoe, Woodbury, Yealmpton.

6. Thirteen dependent on churches outside the diocese: Abbotskerswell, Beer (with Seaton), Littleham (Exmouth), Newton St Petrock and Hollacombe (both dedicated to St Petrock and belonging to the priests of Bodmin); Northam, Otterdon, Ottery St Mary, Revelstoke, Roridge (in Upottery), Umberleigh, Uplyme, Yarcombe.

7. Tavistock Abbey and nine dependents: Abbotsham, Brentor, Burrington, Coffinswell, Denbury, Hatherleigh, Milton Abbot, Plymstock, St Giles on the Heath.

8. Buckfast Abbey and six dependents: Churchstow, Down St Mary; Petrockstow and South Brent (both dedicated to St Petrock); Trusham, Zeal Monachorum.

9. Modbury Priory.

10. To the above must be added some thirty others whose dedication to the early Celtic saints confirm their pre-Conquest origin. Doubt must be cast, however, on Ashcombe (St Nectan) as this would appear to be too far distant from Barnstaple Bay and St Nectan's journeyings into Cornwall; and Harford (St Petrock)—Brooking-Rowe gives St Patrick and Oliver no dedication at all. Exeter; St Kerrian's, St Petrock's, St David's, St Paul's, St Cuthbert's. Ashcombe, Bradstone (dedicated to St Nonne, a Cornish saint). Bridgerule, Charles, Clannaborough, Coryton, Dartmouth, Dunkeswell, East Portlemouth (dedicated to St Winwaloe, of Cornish-Breton origin). Filleigh, Harford, Instow, Kenton (now All Saints but originally, says Polwhele, dedicated to St Petrock, though he gives no authority for the statement), Landkey, Lewtrenchard, Lundy, Lydford, Okehampton, Parracombe, Petton (Bampton), Romansleigh, St Budeaux, Tamerton Foliot, Tormohun, Welcombe, West Anstey.

11. Finally, seven churches whose foundation is uncertain but was probably pre-Conquest: Bere Ferrers, Hawkchurch, Ipplepen, Marystow, Pyworthy, Ugborough, Whitchurch.

Braunton. Notable for its wide nave, bench ends and unusual chancel-arch screen

3. Norman

At the time of the Domesday survey, Devon was one of the most populous counties in England. Though there were still only five large borough towns—Exeter, Totnes, Barnstaple, Lydford and Okehampton—its population included 17,434 men and only Lincolnshire, Norfolk and Suffolk surpassed it in numbers.

With the arrival of the Norman conquerors, the

Branscombe. From the south-east.
The transept was added in the thirteenth century

diocese of Exeter—which, until 1876, included Cornwall—embarked upon a widespread programme of church building. The Norman masons gave their orders and labourers toiled in village and hamlet, sometimes on churches which would serve only a few isolated farmsteads. No doubt, too, that by the end of the period, c 1120-60, many of these masons included native-born men who had been trained up in the Norman-Romanesque traditions. Although much of the work of these Norman masons has since been destroyed in later restorations, many of which involved complete rebuilding, there is still evidence of Norman masonry in about eighty Devon churches.

A fully developed style when first imported into England, Norman architecture reached its highest stage of perfection simultaneously on both sides of the Channel. Using stone that was easy to work and employing granite only for the more roughly-hewn fonts, the Norman masons constructed arcades with massive round or octagonal piers, cushion capitals and semicircular arches, sometimes highly enriched with chevron and billet ornament. They fashioned round-headed windows, round-headed doors; or placed square-headed ones under a round arch, the space between the lintel and the arch being called the tympanum.

The plan of the Norman Devon church was usually either cruciform, comprising a nave, a chancel of the same width and height, and small north and south transepts, or with an unaisled nave and chancel. Occasionally, as at Aveton Giffard, Brentor, Haccombe, Honeychurch, West Down and West Ogwell, the early plan is preserved complete. Sometimes we find an aisle along one side of the nave and a transept off the other, an indication that the aisle was added at a later date; as at Cookbury (north aisle Perpendicular), where nearly the whole of the small original edifice survives. Aisled churches of this period were, however, built in Devon, as at St Mary Arches, Exeter; Farway, Hawkchurch, Mariansleigh, Membury, Salcombe Regis and Sidbury.

Towers were central, low and massive, as at Branscombe and also at Sidbury, which was accurately rebuilt and had a spire added in the restoration of 1884. Occasionally, as at Ilfracombe, the towers are found in the north transeptal position, an arrangement particularly favoured in north Devon. The walls of naves and chancels were sometimes as much as four feet thick, and the masonry at the base of towers even six feet thick, again as at Ilfracombe. Squared stones were used, with wide mortar joints in the earlier work but narrower in work dating from around 1120.

This was a period marked by a great religious revival, during which the parochial system was perfected and parish boundaries drawn. It was also the beginning of the organised English Church and henceforward ecclesiastical history becomes very much a part of the history of these islands, best symbolized perhaps by our fonts where, for centuries, our forebears were brought within a short time of their birth. They have always stood close to the entrance to our churches and are still the first objects to attract attention. Often, too, the font is the only remaining link with the builders who crossed from Normandy.

Over 140 fonts of this period (1066-1189) have survived in Devon and they occupy a pre-eminent place among the fonts of England. Several are claimed to be pre-Conquest, but the only one of which this is unquestionably true is at Dolton, where part of a tenth-century Saxon Christian monument was adapted for use as a font by the Normans. Set upon a modern pedestal, it consists of two blocks, one square with elaborate and well-preserved interlacing on all sides, the other—which has been turned upside down and hollowed out—tapering with Celtic inter-twisted symmetrical animals, a human head with moustaches growing into animals and also interlacing. Of the rest, the cylindrical font at Exeter, St Mary Steps, is undoubtedly one of the earliest.

The majority of these fonts are tall and mounted, usually either circular or square, and only one, at Bradford, is oval. Decoration is rich and diverse, with palmette friezes and running scrolls (Farringdon), rosettes in circles (Combe-in-Teignhead), grotesque faces (Tetcott), and incised dragons (Dean Prior). South-west Devon must have been furnished with fonts made at the same period by the same artificers, as no less than seventeen circular red sandstone fonts occur in the deaneries of Moretonhampstead, Woodleigh, Totnes and Plympton, eleven of them ornamented with the honeysuckle design. The font at Stoke Canon, an early example, is square, decorated with figures and beasts, and was fashioned from a single block of lava. 'Very strange and archaic,' wrote Francis Bond. At South Milton the decoration incorporates cable and zigzag mouldings, depicting two animals and a woman falling backwards—the meaning of which is not clear.

The twelfth-century fonts of Alphington, Dunkeswell, Luppitt and Poltimore are of particular interest. The one at Poltimore is simply a stone bucket with a pair of roll mouldings set close

Exeter, St Mary Steps. Cylindrical foot with crude palmette scroll

together, encircling it midway. This type of font is known as a 'girdled tub' and another fine example is to be seen at Bere Ferrers. The Alphington font, considered by many to be the finest in Devon, is of Beer stone. It is circular, with intersecting arches and a band of scroll roundels depicting St Michael, the dragon, an archer and other figures. Luppitt's font, by contrast, is barbaric, square, and shows a centaur carrying a spear and fighting two dragons, a group of dachshund-like beasts facing each other with grinning jaws, and two men fighting with large, nail-shaped clubs. Were they all mere figments of the artist's imagination?

At Dunkeswell, the waist of the tub is contracted and around it runs a waistband of interlacings. Crude figures in arcades of columns include a bishop, a doctor, and an elephant—possibly the earliest English representation of this animal.

Of granite fonts, the most notable is that of Lustleigh; its central support, one of seven, may, at one time, have been an independent font. Other good granite examples are at Bratton Clovelly, Bridgerule (an elementary shape resembling an egg-cup without any pronounced structural articulation), Down St Mary and Woodleigh.

Often members of a Norman church are repro-

Luppitt. Norman font of the most barbaric 'native' kind

duced decoratively, examples of which can be seen in the following churches:

(i) String courses, usually semicircular rolls: Bickington, Bideford, Hartland, South Brent.

(ii) Arcading: Alphington, Crediton (square, shallow bowl of Purbeck marble).

(iii) Shafts, usually cylindrical: Hartland, Highampton, Netherexe.

(iv) Capitals: Buckfastleigh, Ilfracombe (Ham Hill stone, re-cut nineteenth century), Molland.

Though no example of a complete Norman church now remains, Branscombe is typical of the period, as well as illustrating the process of gradual development from the eleventh century onwards. Some of the masonry on the inner side of the lower part of the tower walls belongs to the Saxon building, and a number of dressed stones, bearing the unmistakable marks of zigzag tooling, have also been re-used in the upper stages. The date of the nave is proved by its corbel-table, and the one-time priest's room in the central chamber of the tower is of special interest, being one of only fourteen remaining in the country.

The only example of Norman arcades on both sides is at St Mary Arches, Exeter (c 1150). There are four bays, circular piers with scalloped capitals, and the arches are double-chamfered. Hawkchurch, too, retains much of this period; notably the chancel arch and north arcade with its square scalloped capitals. The south arcade is Early English with uncommonly fine leaf capitals, interspersed

South Brent. Norman tower, originally on the crossing; the rest c 1436

with little figures: a man with a dog, a man with bagpipes, etc. The exterior of this church was renewed and a new chancel built in 1862. Scalloped capitals are also to be seen on the massive early piers of Farway's north arcade, and at Colebrooke the blocked, round-headed arches of the outside south wall of the nave once formed an arcade between the nave and the south aisle of this twelfth-century church. Inside, the arch near the pulpit shows that a south transept existed before the present one.

Important Norman towers are at Ilfracombe, Loxbeare, Sidbury and South Brent. At South Brent, what was the original crossing tower—as survives at Branscombe and Sidbury—has become the west tower of a later church. At Axminster, Colyton and Crediton, whose churches have otherwise been entirely rebuilt, the towers have been reconstructed or heightened above the older arches of the crossing. And, venerable though the thirteenth-century arches at Axminster and Colyton

are, they superseded still earlier ones in the same position. Similarly replacing an earlier fabrication, and unusual in the county, is Colyton's late fifteenth-century octagonal lantern, imposed upon the stump of the old.

The four-pointed arches of Crediton go back a century earlier and rest on massive piers whose shafts are decorated with such typical Norman ornaments as birds, snakes, zigzag and scallop mouldings. The second floor—the ringing loft—has lancet windows with circular heads and above it is the bell chamber, retaining Early English characteristics in contrast to the parapet and pinnacles which are Perpendicular.

Norman doorways can be seen in forty Devon churches, the best examples being at Axmouth, East Worlingham, Loxbeare, Shebbear, Woolsery and Parkham. At Worlingham, the outer arch moulding with zigzag rests on a beast's head on the left, and there are three inner arch bands of saltire crosses. Loxbeare is notable for the outer zigzag

Bishopsteignton: west portal.
Showing beak-heads, a favourite
with the Norman carver

moulding of jambs and arch, while Shebbear's south doorway is probably the most ambitious in the county, with one order of colonettes and three orders of arch voussoirs, including beakheads and zigzag. Shebbear, Woolsery and Parkham, all situated in the same area and of much the same period (1160-75), are so very similar as to suggest the work of the same master mason.

Shobrooke's south doorway, built of Thorverton stone from Raddon, is also of special interest, while at Mortehoe the doorway connecting the tower (c 1260) in the north position to the nave was once the entry into an earlier building of rectangular plan. The arch here, in two semi-circular rings—a main and a sub-arch—is plain and of characteristically bold Norman style.

So highly valued were these doorways that many were preserved and moved when extensions were made, as at Buckland Filleigh, Knowstone, Lapford, Thorverton, Southleigh, Whitchurch and St Peter's, Tiverton. In most places they are the only remnant of the earlier building, though at Lapford the door itself is possibly also Norman. Original stonework was, of course, often re-used by later builders, as in the archway of the south porch of Clovelly (built c 1450), whose plain pattern carried out in readed lines is evidence of early Norman zigzag work.

Lavishly decorated tympana are rare in Devon and unquestionably the finest example is to be seen at Bishopsteignton. Now built into the south wall, it belonged to a south doorway long since walled up, and represents the Adoration of the Magi. A twelfth-century tympanum at Down St Mary—the sole remnant of the Norman building—depicts Daniel in the Lion's Den, while another at Loxbeare (south doorway) is believed by Cresswell to be the original and the name 'AILMA REECIT' carved on it to be that of its mason.

Piscinas are not easy to date but there are at least five of the Norman period in Devon, including the richly-carved pillar piscina at Luppitt, the bowl of which bears the head of a man with leaves coming from his mouth.

Other authenticated remains of the Norman period and the churches in which they may be seen include the following:

(i) Chancel masonry: Axmouth, Dowland, Paignton, Upton Hellions.

(ii) North chancel windows: Brushford, Clawton, Coldridge.

(iii) Nave masonry (south walls): Axmouth, Instow, Marystow, Pancrasweek.

(iv) Nave masonry (north wall lower part): Broadwoodwidger, possibly also lower wall of north transept.

(v) North nave windows: Meeth.

(vi) Chancel arch (north pier only): Meavy.

(vii) Chancel arch: Witheridge.

(viii) Vestry arch (originally occupying a different site): Berrynarbor.

(ix) South transept masonry: Woolsery.

Thus, Norman workmanship is by no means lost in Devon, an enduring reminder of the great activity of the Norman masons whose influence was felt even to the birth of Perpendicular Gothic some 200 years later.

Bishopsteignton: tympanum. Now built into the south wall, and all that remains of the Norman south doorway

4. Early English

Primarily because it is so overshadowed by succeeding styles, thirteenth-century church building in Devon is a comparatively neglected study. Yet the long, narrow lancet windows, the slender, lofty, pointed arches and spires of the period are still to be seen, though the richly-moulded Early Gothic door is unfortunately rare and there is little remaining evidence of the increased delicacy in ornamentation brought about by the introduction of the chisel.

Also, the backwaters of Devon and Cornwall were slow to abandon the earlier forms, their churches continuing to retain a strong 'Norman' flavour over a 'period lag' which had its effect throughout the region. Such work of the period as remains is largely due to the exceptional activity of Bishop Walter Bronescombe (1258-80) in consecrating new churches and rebuilding old ones. In

Aveton Giffard: *c* 1250-1300.
Bombed during the second world war and since rebuilt

1259 alone he was responsible for the addition of forty parish churches, and within ten years the number had grown to eighty-eight.

Much was learnt from the monastic church-builders, and some of their churches, such as Tavistock (974) and Buckfast (1030) were, architecturally, more important than the parish churches. Other monastic houses followed in the twelfth and thirteenth centuries, and the remains of three of these are still to be found at Buckland (1278), Frithelstock (c 1250) and Torre (c 1180).

The best surviving examples of Early Gothic or Early English church architecture in Devon are at Aveton Giffard (despite much rebuilding after extensive bomb damage in 1943), Branscombe, Braunton, Brentor, Buckerell, Exeter (St Pancras), Ottery St Mary, Pilton, Ringmore and West Ogwell.

Aveton Giffard, says Pevsner, is both unusual and spatially satisfying. A grant of some £30,000 from the War Damage Commission made possible the almost complete rebuilding of the tower roof and chancel in conformity with what is believed to have been the original design, though Oliver in 1840 claimed that excavation had shown the crossing tower to be built on top of the wall of a still earlier building. The building dates essentially from 1250-1300 and the arches of the tower are on three strong shafts, each with moulded capitals. The north wall of the nave has single lancet windows, while the east chancel window incorporates elaborate geometrical tracery with circles containing cinquefoils and others containing secondary foiled inner circles. Neither the fifteenth-century north chancel aisle nor the fourteenth-century south

Shaldon (Ringmore): thirteenth-century chapel. Rebuilt 1622, and interior renewed 1894

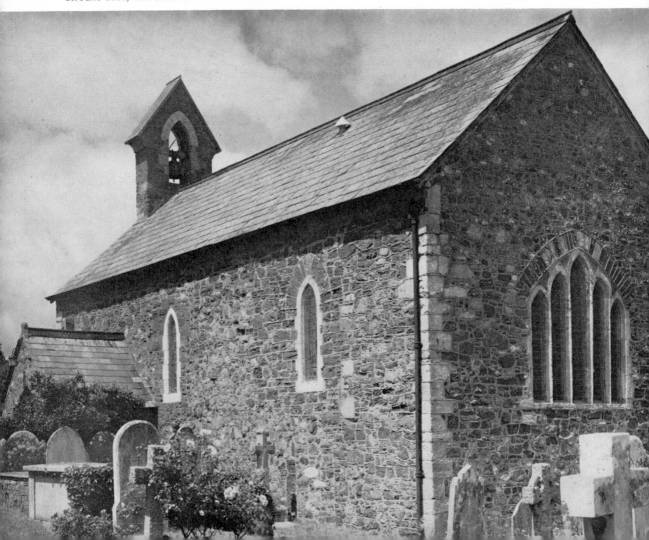

chancel aisle have been rebuilt.

The circular turret with conical roof on the south-west has been rebuilt and gives access to the ringing loft. It is in the same Norman style as the vanished turrets of Bishopsteignton, East Teignmouth and St Mary Major, Exeter, and it would seem from available data that Devon towers of the twelfth century and earlier stood in an axial position over the choir between sanctuary and nave, without transepts, as at Branscombe. The porch, the only part of Aveton Giffard which survived the bombing, has an outer doorway with three orders and an inner doorway with one. The latter, leading into the nave, has a double set of arches on the inner side. Prior to the bombing, there was a good example of an Early English double piscina in the south wall of the chancel.

An all-round early church is rare in Devon and the one at Ringmore, although restored in 1862-3, is still a fine architectural example. Primitive, both in type and workmanship, it is of the aisleless cruciform type, in which the south transept is represented by a transeptal tower. The exterior is more interesting than the interior, which has been rather spoilt by tawdry Victorian decoration. Some of the windows have been renewed, but no window details are later than c 1300, featuring lancets with plain-pointed or pointed trefoil heads. In the east wall of the transept are two small round-headed lights, with jambs and heads of thin voussoirs and divided by a massive buttress of rubble masonry. Characteristic of those in this locality is the late thirteenth-century embattled tower. Low, with lancet windows, it has a tiny spire and diagonal buttresses at the foot only. Inside the south porch there is a pointed tunnel-vault of the Decorated period. The chancel arch and that of the transept are both apparently late thirteenth century, again of simple, almost primitive design. Indeed, throughout the entire building there is nothing in the way of mouldings, shafts or decorative devices to suggest the distinctive Early English period.

Braunton tower, rather short and stunted, was built about 1250, in the south transept position. It is topped by a broach spire—one of three in north Devon, the others being at Barnstaple (St Peter's)

Mortehoe: mainly thirteenth century. Thought to have been founded by Sir William de Tracey in 1170

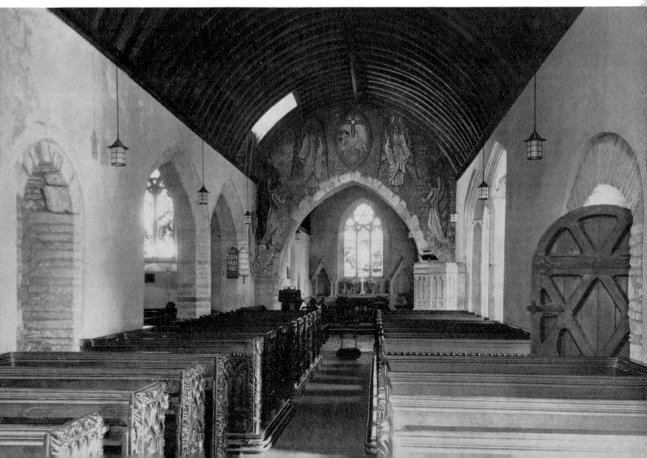

and Swimbridge—which rises to a height of 118 ft. The transeptal towers of East Down and Yarnscombe (built in the north position, as was the Norman tower of Ilfracombe) are of the same date. Braunton is built on an unusual plan. The nave is wide—34 ft—and indications of extensive thirteenth-century re-building are afforded by the chancel arch, the arch on the south (leading from the nave into the present lady chapel) and the lancet window in the equivalent position on the north. Was the Norman nave perhaps narrower, and bordered on the north and south by two narrow aisles?

Salcombe Regis church was built by the Normans, and remains of that period include the circular piers of the north arcade, with circular scalloped capitals, and the mangled stones of a doorway in the south chancel wall. Later—a dedication date of 1259 is recorded—Bishop Bronescombe had the chancel lengthened and a south aisle built—work which can be seen to this day.

Meavy is another example of a Norman church which was reconstructed at this period. Grants, under the family name of de Mewi, to the religious houses of Plympton and Buckland, c 1202 and 1214, are extant, but the individuals cannot be identified. The chancel was extended, a new east window incorporated, and some authorities have also claimed Meavy's unbuttressed west tower for this period. Cornelius, however, sounds a note of caution in dating any structure in Devon unless it has either definite architectural features or documentary evidence on which to base a conclusion, and even this can be dangerous as the dedication ceremony is not necessarily the date of the structure. Denbury, for instance, is referred to in the 'Taxation of Pope Nicholas' as having been completed in 1291, and while this date accords with the architectural characteristics of the present chancel (the windows are a good example of early intersecting bar tracery), Bishop Stapledon's register states that Denbury and its high altar were not dedicated until 27 August 1318. And in the case of Meavy, whilst the rectangular form of the stair turret indicates an early date, the base course is formed of granite, which was never used in large quantities prior to the Perpendicular period. This alone would appear to confirm its medieval origin.

Exeter, St Pancras, consisting of nave and chancel, bears evidence of greater antiquity than almost any church in Exeter, says Stabb. Certainly the font is the oldest in the city—massive and circular, with elementary Norman decoration of

pellet moulding round the top. The chancel, too, has some old windows (renewed in 1888 by Pearson who also built the Gothic chancel arch); the east is a lancet of three lights with trefoiled head; on the north side is one of two lights and a single lancet. On the south side there is a piscina with pointed trefoil arch.

In the pre-Perpendicular era it is not always easy, particularly in the poorer districts, to determine Early English, but at Buckerell the transepts, plain unbuttressed west tower and absence of aisles would all seem to indicate c 1250. At Holne, with marked batter, the tower is the only survival of the early medieval church, and the same can be said of Morleigh. Copeland claims sixty-four towers as evidence of thirteenth-century work, and these sometimes incorporate diagonal buttresses at the foot, as at Diptford, Malborough, North Huish, Rattery and Blackawton, which also has the early stair-turret much favoured by Perpendicular church-builders in the southern part of the county.

The towers at Diptford and Malborough are topped by broach spires—another adornment much favoured in the South Hams—which were added later. Malborough spire was damaged by lightning in 1829, taken down and rebuilt. Early unbuttressed towers with stair-turrets are to be seen at Bickleigh (near Tiverton) and Broadhempston (c 1280). A very plain Early English tower is that of West Teignmouth. Of one stage, it is built of red conglomerate and has a parapet slightly corbelled (not embattled). There are low plain face buttresses and single bell chamber lights.

West Ogwell, one of the most attractive country churches in Devon, is cruciform and aisleless. Virtually an unaltered building of c 1280, apart from the two-storey unbuttressed tower added about 1320, the windows have tracery intersected and cusped into the shape of pointed trefoils and quatrefoils. In the chancel, a sedilia incorporates three-pointed trefoil heads.

Bradstone and Brentor both exhibit much Early English work. To the Norman nave of Bradstone was added a rebuilt chancel—note its lancet window and single-stage early buttress, a rarity this, since walling was not usually buttressed prior to the fifteenth century. The chancel was possibly slightly lengthened eastward and heightened during the late fifteenth or early sixteenth century. Brentor, situated over 1,100 ft above sea level on the summit of a tor of volcanic origin, is an aisleless rectangle, without structural division between nave and chancel. It affords the unusual example of an Early English roof of single-framed rafter construction and very flat pitch. It is, however, a modern renewal in which the original construction and detail are believed to have been faithfully perpetuated. The masonry suggests alteration or enlargement from an earlier building.

At Pilton, the most interesting part of the church is the ground floor of the tower—in the north, close to the east end. It incorporates a groined entrance from the chancel, with acutely pointed arch, and the remains of a vaulted interior—evidenced by pillars 8 ft 8 in high at each corner and still with their caps and bases intact. This and the north aisle, *c* 1260, formed part of the early church of the priory. Originally, the chancel entrance into the tower was undoubtedly an exterior feature—note the plinth at the floor projecting about three inches but cut away on the chancel side to give a plain surface. The western arch is open, with the organ beneath, and beyond the eastern arch, now walled up, stood the chancel of the priory church. Just above the belfry floor the interior is octagonal, carried on squint arches, and continues thus up to the bottom of the bell windows, where it becomes a square. The octagonal plan of this older portion indicates that it may originally have carried an octagonal spire, shorter but similar to the broached spires of nearby St Peter's, Barnstaple, and Braunton. The whole tower was much restored in 1696.

The priory cloisters were along the north wall of the north aisle, and the three-light, square-headed Tudor windows (note the high sills) now in this wall were originally in the cloisters and were probably built just before the suppression of the monasteries. The roof-line of adjoining priory buildings can be seen on the north wall of the tower and shows that they must have been extensive and of considerable height. The roof of the north aisle was raised in 1639. A lancet window in the west wall of the tower, now blocked up, shows below the roof and would formerly have been outside and overlooking the old roof, which was probably of the steep 'span' type. At that time the aisle was the nave of the Early English church and its south wall, now pierced by unmoulded pointed arches, would have had narrow lancet windows requiring the arcading to be virtually cut out of the solid wall. The present nave and chancel were entirely constructed about 1320.

Notable examples of Bishop Bronescombe's work can be seen at Ottery St Mary and Branscombe, two 'showpiece' churches upon which he lavished much care and attention. Those surviving at Ottery St Mary include the side aisles of the chancel with lancet windows and the lower two-thirds of the transeptal towers—note also the groups of five lancet windows in the east walls of the transepts.

West Ogwell:
cruciform and aisleless, *c* 1280.
Tower added in 1320

The church itself was consecrated on Thursday 4 December 1259, and it was not until some seventy-five years later that the parish church of 'St Marie de Otery' was converted into a collegiate foundation—a church which vies with Crediton for second place in Devon. The cathedral at Exeter and Ottery St Mary are the only two churches in England where the transepts are formed of towers; the latter is a copy of Exeter, where the arrangement was introduced into the twelfth-century building.

Walter Bronescombe is known to have visited his native parish of Branscombe on at least two occasions. The nave was lengthened and the transepts built between 1250 and 1260 but only the simple lancet windows of the north transept now remain; the south window doubtless matched it but was replaced in the fifteenth century by the present window. It is interesting to note that the transepts were added to the west of the crossing tower instead of branching out from it. This could have been to avoid interfering with the stair-turret, although there are instances where the turret has been modified to incorporate at least a part of it in an arm of the transept, but it is more likely here that the position was dictated by the nature of the ground.

There are other notable survivals of this early period in various parts of the county which can best be listed alphabetically:

Brentor: the church on top of the tor.
A landmark for many miles around

Abbotskerswell:	chancel		porating pointed trefoil head and double piscina with a blank quatrefoil
Ashcombe:	tower (dedicated 1259)		
Axminster:	piers of crossing tower; west parts of chancel masonry	Lydford:	chancel (dedication date 1261)
Axmouth:	south aisle	Martinhoe:	tower and chancel
Bere Ferrers:	tower	Marwood:	chancel and south transept
Berrynarbor:	chancel—with pointed trefoil headed piscina	Membury:	lancet windows
		Morebath:	tower (lower part)
Broadhempston:	tower and chancel (chancel windows nineteenth century)	Mortehoe:	chancel
		Newton Tracey:	tower and windows
Broadwoodwidger:	chancel and tower arch	North Tawton:	tower
Buckfastleigh:	tower arch	Offwell:	chancel arch
Butterleigh:	tower	Parracombe:	chancel
Cheriton Bishop:	chancel	St Giles on the Heath:	chancel
Chudleigh:	tower		
Clannaborough:	tower	Sampford Peverell:	lancet windows; north arcade, moulded capitals; dedicated 1259
Cofton:	masonry; in ruins, eighteenth century, vastly restored 1838-9		
		Shaldon (Ringmore):	thirteenth-century chapel
Combe Martin:	chancel		
Cornwood:	tower	Stockleigh Pomeroy:	lancet windows; tower arch; dedicated 1259
Coryton:	chancel		
Dartmouth, St Saviour:	first two bays, nave arcade	Tetcott:	windows
		Thurlestone:	lancet windows; double-headed piscina incorporating pointed trefoil niches with a pierced, pointed quatrefoil above
East Ogwell:	chancel		
Ermington:	steeple		
Hawkchurch:	south side arcade		
Hemyock:	tower		
Hollacombe:	tower	West Worlington:	tower (lower part)
Kingsbridge:	crossing tower	Whitchurch:	chancel
Luppitt:	chancel	Willand:	tower
Lustleigh:	chancel—with sedilia incor-		

Axmouth: much Norman work.
The south aisle was added c 1250

Ermington: late thirteenth-century steeple,
the rest mainly fourteenth century

5. Decorated

It took eighty-five years, beginning in 1295, to build the cathedral of St Mary and St Peter at Exeter. Though its main design was determined before that date, credit for much of the work belongs to Walter de Stapledon (1308-26) and John de Grandisson (1326-69), two bishops whose munificence and genius were instrumental in raising many new places of religious worship and in reconstructing others. Their occupancy of the see coincided with what is known as the Decorated Gothic period, which was also the time of a general increase in the wealth of the county. Devon's importance architecturally began to increase, although its churches were still restrained in

Exeter Cathedral: choir.
Started in 1275; the chancel
completed c 1309

decoration and the tracery of the period generally unpopular.

Even in the cathedral, the tracery does not begin to take to flowing forms, and then reluctantly, until after about 1330. Rare, too, is even such a restrained form of it as the ogee reticulation motif, though examples are to be found at Clayhanger, Farway, Milton Damerel, Mortehoe, Tawstock, West Down and at Dittisham (consecrated *de novo constructum* in 1333). At Ottery St Mary, by contrast, there is a complete absence of tracery in the eight-light east window of the lady chapel.

Design, at least in the early part of the period, is influenced by Exeter, as witness the lavish five-light window of Plympton St Mary with its six-pointed star in a circle, and the fine sedilia and piscina in its fourteenth-century chancel. Ornament shows more refinement but less strength and vigour. Towers do not differ a great deal from Early English; only twenty-four, according to Copeland, are Decorated.

No more than seven Devon churches can be considered unquestionably fourteenth-century buildings. Of these, Haccombe and Ottery St Mary take pride of place, though none the less interesting are Bratton Clovelly, Milton Damerel, Modbury, Morleigh and Tawstock. Bishops Tawton and Bere

Ferrers also exhibit a number of Decorated features and Woodleigh, too, with its early plan—cruciform with low unbuttressed west tower—could be of this period, despite its lack of ornament. Unfortunately, it was drastically 'restored' in 1891, leaving little of architectural interest.

Haccombe, dedicated in 1328 and one of the smallest parishes in England, is probably an example of a belated dedication several years after the building had been completed. The first structure was probably an unaisled rectangle built late in the twelfth century, followed a hundred years later by a complete remodelling and the addition of a north aisle. The date of this north aisle is not easy to ascertain—though most in this position are early and much less ornate than aisles built to the south. The short, sturdy, octagonal, red sandstone piers of small-jointed masonry and broad unmoulded arches indicate *c* 1310, though the octagonal plan for piers was used throughout the whole of the Gothic period and is not, in itself, a sure indication of date. A more reliable guide, which would seem to confirm the suggested date, is the very elementary form of the capitals. The whole interior is rather dark, as our churches were at this time, and though much has been renewed since its thirteenth-century remodelling, it has not been extended. Today, it is

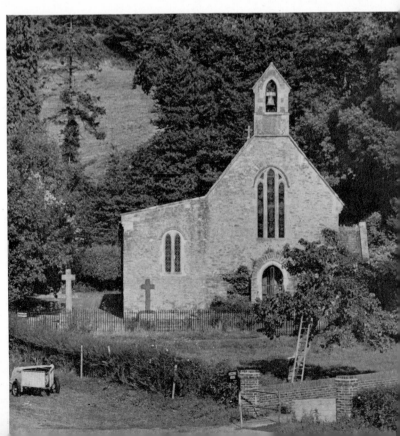

Haccombe: consecrated by Bishop Grandisson in 1328. Since renewed but not enlarged

notable for its brasses and effigies, which are among the finest in the county.

Grandisson's greatest achievement was the rebuilding of Ottery St Mary. It was completed in 1342 and the greater part, including the tops of the transeptal towers (71 ft), nave and chancel (each five bays) and lady chapel, must be assigned to this date. Its belated severity of style was the result of trying to reconcile the need for a large cathedral-like edifice with the limited funds that could be spared from the costly work in progress at Exeter. The parapets were much restored in 1826 and again in 1872, and the corbel table of each tower carries seven lions' heads as gargoyles on the three outer faces. The spire on the north tower, similar to the one on Exeter Cathedral until 1752, was completely dismantled in 1908, when a new framework was erected, using the old lead.

The weathercock, known as the 'Whistling Cock' or 'Trumpeting Cock', is reputed to be the oldest *in situ* in Europe. It has two tubes in the base, and the wind, blowing through these, made a weird moaning sound until silenced at the turn of the century after the parishioners had complained about the noise. The square, two-storied vestries on either side of the choir aisles, somewhat out of keeping with the general plan and unlike anything else in the diocese, were added by Grandisson.

The chancel ceiling is richly groined with diagonal moulded ribs formed into small quatrefoil panels. Strikingly bold in design, and intended solely as ornamentation, these ribs are similar in arrangement to those at Wells Cathedral, where John de Grandisson was canon and prebendary from 1306 until 1326. Rarely did fourteenth-century masons attempt such work, much preferring ogee arches to curves in vaulting, and Pevsner quotes this example as one of the few cases in England in which the curvilinear spirit has penetrated into the vault. The figured roof bosses of the lady chapel are also notable, and were probably the work of the carvers responsible for the nave vault at Exeter. The choir resembles the eastern limb of Bristol Cathedral where the work was carried out under Abbot Knowle from 1306 to 1322.

Ottery St Mary is typical of the change which commenced a hundred years earlier and which can be seen in many of our cathedrals and larger churches. The composition was changing from heavy to light, from low to lofty, from horizontal to vertical; there is vigour and boldness, combined with a lightness, characteristic of a greater freedom of thought and of action.

The reredos, *c* 1342-5 and restored by Blore in 1833, has four buttresses with figure niches framing three nodding ogee niches and steep cusped gables. The top has massive mouldings and incorporates ten shields. The richly-canopied stone sedilia is of much the same date—they were at their finest during this period—but not to be compared with the one at Blackawton, which is perhaps the best of all. Other notable remains of Grandisson's work include the misericords in the lady chapel and chancel, the parclose screens, and the gilded wooden lectern in the form of an eagle, one of the earliest of the twenty wooden medieval lecterns now remaining in England. The parclose screens, though not in their correct position, are historically interesting as being amongst the earliest wooden screens preserved in Devon (*c* 1350). They have straight tops and cusped ogee arches, and above each there is a circle with an ogee trefoil. An ancient clock in the south transept is attributed to Grandisson, but

Ottery St Mary: chancel and nave *c* 1337-42. Chancel vault is one of the finest in England

is more probably a fifteenth-century copy of the original. Similar clocks are to be found at Exeter, Wimborne Minster and Wells.

Bratton Clovelly is a complete rebuilding of an earlier cruciform aisleless building. The chancel, with its early fourteenth-century windows, chancel arch, nave arcades, and lofty tower arch, are all of this period. Excavation to the west of the tower would probably uncover the foundations of its former nave, and to the north, its north transept. The tower, of two periods, is a Perpendicular rebuilding using granite, and the absence of buttresses or a west door indicates an early date. On the north, a large pointed arch is blocked and a roof line above it shows clearly that a north transept once existed. The west wall of the north aisle appears to be of earlier masonry and is possibly the east wall of the north transept, just as the west wall of the south aisle may be the remains of the west wall of the south transept. The presence of a short and deeply splayed lancet in the latter wall indicates late twelfth century. The piers of the south arch of the tower, the lower courses of the tall main tower-arch, with their characteristic stops, and the plain square plinths of the arcade piers, also appear to be early remains. Part of the present nave may, therefore, have originally been the chancel.

Milton Damerel is notable for its windows. Restoration came late (1892-1904) and was carefully carried out. Essentially, it is early medieval (c 1300-25), its chancel with south window still geometrical (cinquefoils) though with pointed

Blackawton: sedilia and piscina. Belonging to the dedication of 1333. Among the finest remaining in the county

trefoil lights, and its east window with ogee reticulation. Its west tower, narrower than the nave and without buttresses, door or pinnacles, was rebuilt with old materials during the restoration. A north aisle was added during the sixteenth century.

Much of Modbury, including the transepts, is Decorated. The piers are thick and short with odd, bevelled capitals, as at Haccombe. The spire was struck by lightning in 1621 but still accurately represents its early fourteenth-century predecessor. The hardly recognizable effigies in the transepts—possibly of the Champernowne family—are also of this date. At Morleigh, the unbuttressed tower is probably Early English, while the nave and south aisle, with plain capitals adorning the arcade, are a

century later. According to Risdon, it is said that during the reign of Edward I, Sir Peter Fishacre, who owned lands in the adjoining parish of Woodleigh, killed the Woodleigh parson in the course of a violent quarrel. Summoned to appear in Rome, he was ordered to do pennance by building Morleigh church, in the chancel of which he is buried.

Tawstock is architecturally one of the most interesting of Devon churches. Its genuine fourteenth-century structural work, combined with one of the most notable collections of monuments in England, gives a rare impression of unspoilt early medieval beauty. It was erected c 1330 with a tall tower, nearly 77 ft to the top of the battlements, over the crossing. A century and a half later

Milton Damerel: c 1300-1325. Famed for its windows of the Decorated period

Barnstaple, St Peter: unusually placed
thirteenth-century tower topped by a lead-covered broach spire

the nave aisles were raised though not widened. In 1540, the chancel aisle was built, and little has since been altered. The end windows of the transepts have ogee reticulation, typical of the second quarter of this period and similar to the north transept, three-light window at West Down. They are constructed in the attractive yellow oolite stone from Ham Hill in Somerset. The east window has an octofoil above three cusped lights and the chancel north windows are in the same style.

Pevsner suggests that the Decorated church-builders pierced earlier walls at Tawstock to add the aisles, the core of the present plan being Norman. The arcades, the arches between nave and chancel, and the nave and transepts are all built in such a way that solid, unmoulded chunks of masonry are left standing, the shallow mouldings being only applied superficially. Interesting, and unlike anything else in the county, is the line of demarcation showing in the exterior of the walling of the west end of the nave south aisle, between the fifteenth-century raised portion and the Decorated walling below. This clearly shows that the nave and aisles were originally under one roof. Over each pier, in both aisles, remain corbel-heads which supported the tie beams or struts of the original roof bosses. In the nave, where the main arches spring from the piers, the sub-arches of each bay finish on to carved corbels, fine specimens of the 'natural' Decorated type of work and carved mainly with human faces and oak leaves.

Although much restored, West Down should not be overlooked. The chancel was rebuilt in 1675, the tower in 1712, and the whole restored in 1874. Plain cruciform in plan, without aisles, the nave and transepts are c 1320, and in the north transept, below the three-light window, a low tomb recess contains a life-size timber effigy of Sir John Stowford, who founded a chantry in this church about the middle of the fourteenth century. A fine pointed cinquefoil-cusped piscina of the same date is now in the chancel, having originally been in the east wall of the north transept. The roof of this transept is unusual. It is late Decorated, built of oak, and the curved braces, instead of being in 'cradle' form, are brought into trefoil outline.

Stoke Gabriel :
tower c 1350. Remainder rebuilt
in the fifteenth century on typical
fully-aisled plan

Bishops Tawton was one of the many churches reconstructed to the orders of Bishop Stapleton who, in August 1316, pronounced it sombre and dilapidated, and its chancel too narrow and dark. The nave, chancel arch, tower in north transeptal position with two-light east window, and spire, all date from this rebuilding. The north aisle is Perpendicular and the chancel itself was rebuilt in 1866. A unique feature of the crocketed octagonal stone spire, 70 ft high, is that the crockets spring directly from the solid masonry and not from the usual cylindrical ribs. The nave wagon roof is original, with plastered panels, moulded ribs and carved bosses.

Ilfracombe is another example of Stapleton's work—in this case an enlargement to accommodate the increasing population. On a visit in November 1321, he ordered the nave be extended by 24 ft and aisles to be added on either side. The construction of the nave arcading necessitated taking down the greater part of the old building. There are four bays on both sides with low octagonal piers and simply chamfered arches. The stone corbels in the nave, fourteen on each side and grotesquely carved in the form of animals and one bird, are of the same date and must have been intended to give support to the trusses of the Decorated roof which preceded the present one. The unwinged figures of angels which they now support are of later date. A piscina in the chancel also dates back to the church's reconstruction, though Hussell, for some unknown reason, ascribes it to about 1450.

Sir William de Ferrers reconstructed Bere Ferrers in about 1333. His effigy, and that of his wife Matilda, can be seen on their canopied tomb in the chancel. In the east window, where they have now been replaced after many vicissitudes, are the fragmentary remains of a fine and elaborate pictorial window from this reconstruction. It is the oldest glass in Devon, apart from one or two windows in Exeter Cathedral, and the colouring still has the glow which later medieval glass so often lacks. The design was possibly influenced by Exeter and is by the same glazier. Among the best preserved panels is a portrait of Sir William dedicating the church, and prominent among the surviving fragments is a panel showing a fine Christ in Majesty.

Reticulated tracery, in Beer stone, can be seen in the end windows of the transepts and in one of the two eastern windows of the north transept. The three-light west window of the north transept is an example of curvilinear tracery, having cinquefoiled main lights, the lateral lights of which are ogee-headed. The south aisle, chancel aisle, and the two-

storeyed south porch with ribbed ceiling are Perpendicular. Though lamentably restored in the mid-nineteenth century, Bere Ferrers remains, nevertheless, both architecturally and archaeologically the most interesting in south-west Devon.

Pyworthy, dedicated by Grandisson in 1334, is of much more ancient foundation. It is mentioned in a charter of Totnes Priory dated 1088 and is the only village church in the diocese possessing an ancient clerestory, part of the early fourteenth-century rebuilding. Also of this period are the octagonal piers and double-chamfered arches of the south arcade, the sedilia and piscina, and the chancel windows. The south aisle and tower are Perpendicular.

Other notable Decorated remains, indicative of the extensive building activity at this time, can be seen at:

Axminster:	chancel windows, sedilia and piscina
Barnstaple, St Peter:	broached lead spire—erected and paid for by the corporation, 1389; restored in the seventeenth century
Bampton:	chancel
Bow:	tower, nave windows
Bradford:	tower
Branscombe:	chancel
Bridford:	chancel (east window original)
Broadclyst:	east window north aisle (unusually fanciful)
Calverleigh:	south aisle
Charleton:	tower
Clawton:	tower, centrally placed polygonal stair-turret in south side, unusual in north Devon
Clovelly:	tower
Colebrooke:	chancel and south transept
Colyton:	east window
Combe Raleigh:	tower
Combe-in-Teignhead:	transepts; high altar dedicated 1339
Crediton:	lady chapel
Dittisham:	chancel
Dolton:	tower
East Ogwell:	transepts
Ermington:	chancel
Exbourne:	east window
Farway:	east window
Harberton:	chancel
Hartland:	nave
Horwood:	chancel
Huish:	tower
Ideford:	arcade

Ilsington:	chancel; east window and north transept window	Shebbear:	south aisle arcade
Kelly:	chancel	Shute:	tower (over crossing)
Kenn:	east window	Sidbury:	east window
Kentisbeare:	chancel and tower	Slapton:	chancel with Decorated windows (dedicated 1318)
Kingston:	chancel; nave with south windows of two lights with a pointed ogee quatrefoil	Stoke Fleming:	arcade
		Stoke Gabriel:	tower
		Swimbridge:	tower
Kings Nympton:	tower (spire renewed, now copper, originally shingled with oak)	Thornbury:	tower (dedicated 1338)
		Townstall (Dartmouth):	arcade (dedicated 1318)
Marystow:	chancel	Ugborough:	nave and aisles (dedicated 1323)
Milton Abbot:	tower		
Netherexe:	chancel	Wembury:	tower
Payhembury:	tower	West Alvington:	chancel
Poltimore:	tower	West Putford:	north transept, chancel and nave windows
Sampford Spiney:	north transept windows; nave		

Hartland : fourteenth-century arcades; enriched ceilings. Roodscreen added *c* 1470

6. Perpendicular

THE GREAT REBUILDING

Very few churches in the county managed to escape rebuilding, or a transformation, which amounted to much the same thing. Then, as today, builders, fascinated by new developments in architecture, delighted in complete renovations and during the period *c* 1377-1547 the stonemason's mastery of his art was such that churches became skeletons in stone with glass between the ribs. Windows were easily distinguishable by the mullions which continued up to the arch, transoms

Alphington : fully-aisled plan with shield-holding angels on pier capitals

were introduced into the tracery, and the period became renowned for the magnificence of its towers, particularly those in the eastern counties and in Somerset and Devon.

This Golden Age of Devon church architecture was largely due to the pressing need for extended naves and additional aisles to accommodate the rapidly growing population, and to the increasingly elaborate forms of ceremonial which could not fittingly be conducted in the dark and narrow village churches of earlier periods. Though slow to gain momentum in the aftermath of the dreaded Black Death, this upsurge of building activity reached its zenith in the last half of the fifteenth century and was most evident in those parishes which had been made prosperous by the cloth industry.

Gothic architecture came late to perfection in Devon, and the markedly Perpendicular architecture of the eastern counties rarely established itself in the Exeter diocese. Nevertheless the county was heir to a vigorous building tradition which survived to a late period, a tradition reflected in its furnishings, especially those of wood, and in a tendency to discard the simpler fittings of earlier times.

The greatest alteration was the virtual elimination of the chancel arch and its replacement, as the crowning glory, by the roodscreen and its loft, a development which eventually led to the almost complete abandonment of the chancel arch as part of the church fabric in the south-western counties. Today, many of these screens—beautiful examples of the woodcarver's art—have been restored and are justly famous.

The characteristic Perpendicular Devon church is an aisled rectangle, planned for an altar at the

Torbryan : the most perfect medieval
interior. Box pews, with candle holders, cover the original benches

east, a tower at the west and a south porch. No doubt because of its greater cost, the clerestory is even rarer than the chancel arch, and only where industry brought wealth, as at Cullompton and Tiverton, was it incorporated into a rebuilding. There was also at this time a strong tendency to retain many motifs associated with the Decorated period—ie, the retention of ogee curves in window tracery—and this may account for the presence of the 'spoke' motif or 'star' tracery in positions where the walling is definitely fifteenth century, as at Ipplepen, Little Hempston, Manaton and Torbryan.

Sometimes construction entailed the dismantling of the middle tower which was not always considered safe. The crossing was then thrown into the nave and a new west tower built, as at Ashburton, Hemyock, and possibly Widecombe-in-the-Moor. The cross plan had gone out of favour, and even when the presence of transepts in a structure indicates fifteenth-century work, as at Ashburton, it is almost certain that a previous building of that form once occupied the site. An exception is Welcombe, in that isolated border country on the Atlantic coast, where north and south transepts were added to the existing structure when the chapel was raised to parochial status in 1508. Occasionally, earlier transepts have been left, as at Buckfastleigh, Combe-in-Teignhead and Paignton, but more often they have been adapted to the reconstructed building. The best examples are at Axminster, Holne, Ilsington (aisles and tower rebuilt in 1480), Rattery, Ugborough (c 1420, when the chancel was also rebuilt), in all of which the transepts have been enlarged into aisles. In the

Chittlehampton : Devon's finest tower of the Perpendicular period, seen from the north-west

north of the county, away from the centres of the cloth trade and so generally less wealthy, reconstruction was not so ambitious. Here, the chancel arches which remain, as at Honeychurch, Mortehoe, Shebbear, Tetcott and Thornbury, are a reflection of poverty, and possibly of less influence by the diocesan powers in Exeter.

Another plan adopted was that of Horwood, where an aisle was added on the north side in 1547, though the south side is still with transept and aisleless. A similar enlargement took place about 1410 at Combe Martin, but here, possibly due to the new riches brought by the silver mines, a short transept was added outside the new north aisle. This resulted in a remarkable show-front with the transept exactly in the centre and the symmetrically arranged north porch further west and the vestry further east. The whole is embattled, the most usual decorative motif where rather more money than usual was available. At Mortehoe, the north transept was enlarged into a short aisle about 1540, and in the more prosperous south, at East Ogwell, Chudleigh and Lustleigh, broad north aisles were added, absorbing the north transepts, whilst south transeptal chapels remained.

The fully aisled plan with the roodscreen extending the full width is, however, the more general plan, and there are many examples of these medieval interiors in Devon, from Hartland in the north to Dartmouth in the south, which compare with the finest this country can offer. Where two aisles were built on to an already existing building, they were often carried right through to the east end of the chancel in the form of chapels separated from the chancel by parclose screens. These enclosures were mostly appropriated as chantry chapels by influential families, or associated with ownership of land,

Ipplepen : of the Totnes type, the tower is 91 feet high, and was constructed in 1440

and good examples of them are the Bagtor and Ingesdon estates at Ilsington, Mowlish and Oxton at Kenton, the Peamore chapel at Exminster, and the Eyston chapel at Morchard Bishop. Among others in Devon are the chantries of the Pole family at Shute, of the Wykes and Burgoynes at South Tawton, and of the Arscotts at Tetcott. Where chapels exist on both sides of the chancel building line, a fine east show front with three large windows is the usual result, as at Milton Abbot, Sutcombe, Tavistock and Plymouth (St Andrew).

The fifteenth-century plan is often found in an incomplete state of development with a single aisle, which is nearly always an addition to an earlier building. Such south-aisle extensions can be seen at Berrynarbor, *c* 1500, Kentisbeare, and at Plymtree, where the west tower was constructed at the same time. North-aisle extensions are more numerous and include Atherington—a surprisingly late addition of 1579—and Down St Mary, where it was included in the rebuilding of 1413 after the destruction of tower and nave in a severe storm. Their construction, particularly in the more rural and less populated parishes, indicates landed wealth.

By far the greatest number of Devon towers were erected during this period, and whilst they may lack the enrichment of their Somerset neighbours, Devon, like most districts where late Gothic archi-

Widecombe-in-the-Moor : claims more visitors than any other Devon parish church. Sometimes called 'the cathedral of the moor'

tecture is prevalent, is still very much a county of towers. In an interesting exercise, Copeland records that of 471 towers surveyed, 423 were in the western position, and that the majority of these had been built or rebuilt during the fifteenth century. Rarely are they other than three-storeyed, with embattled parapets and seldom more than four pinnacles. Of 446 towers considered, 232 have projecting stair-turrets, and of those, 170 are hexagonal or octagonal, 36 rectangular, and six round. The commonest position for the stair-turret is north-east (or north side), of which there are 114 examples. The least common is the south-east (or south side), of which there are only seven. Only Tavistock has north and south arcades for a passageway through the basement. This base dates from the fourteenth century and originally formed one of the abbey gateways, known as the 'Cemetery Gateway' and leading to the abbey which stood immediately to the south of the parish church. Only Plymouth (St Andrew) has fully developed north and south doorways instead of a west doorway and, with Sidbury, are the only two churches to have stone-vaulted basements.

Tower design in Somerset exercised some influence over neighbouring counties, and to it we may attribute the fine tower of Broadclyst, c 1530, Cullompton, completed 1549, and Tiverton, 1520. All three reveal their origin in their parapets and pinnacles, their belfry windows filled with pierced stone tracery, and their broad buttresses. Chittlehampton's tower (c 1480), praised by historians and ecclesiologists alike, is perhaps Devon's finest and, according to Dr Milles in his Parochial Collection, is said 'to be the work of the same architect who built the towers of Gloucester Cathedral and of Probus in Cornwall'. It bears some resemblance to the tower at St Mary's, Taunton, but excels all its neighbours both in richness of decoration—Miss E. K. Prideaux (MSS) describes it as originally having seventy-two pinnacles—and by its striking dimensions. Twenty-five feet square at the base, it is of four stages and rises to a height of 125 ft, including pinnacles. Of the Perpendicular towers, only Hartland (128 ft) and Plymouth, St Andrew (136 ft) are higher. Other impressive towers in north Devon are at Berrynarbor (1480), Combe Martin (late fifteenth century), and Bishops Nympton which, at 100 ft, is the highest in proportion to the square of its base.

The most common type of Devonian tower is more remarkable for its strength and adequacy than for its beauty. Generally, they are plain, austere and, due to the intractability of the local stone, lacking in adornment. Nonetheless, the severely plain outline of such towers as Ashburton, built in 1430 of granite averaging $4\frac{1}{2}$ ft in thickness; of Ipplepen, in 1440, with walls 6 ft thick at base; Kingsteignton in 1480, and Torbryan in 1440, are all impressive examples of late medieval masoncraft. Their impression of height is also much enhanced by the economy in string-courses, which are almost hidden by the coating of rough-cast and the vertical design of the buttresses. The tower at Totnes, whose corner pinnacles are the tallest in the county, is of similar design. Constructed between 1449 and 1459 by master-mason Roger Growdon, it is 25 ft square at the base and 120 ft high.

Granite lends itself well to tower construction and there are many built of this material in the Dartmoor region and to the west and north-west, including Plympton St Mary, 108 ft high; Plymouth, St Andrew, built 1460-65; Walkhampton, Sheepstor, Mary Tavy (early sixteenth century), Peter Tavy, and Ugborough (completed 1520). Widecombe-in-the-Moor's tower, also of granite and said to have been erected as a thank-offering by tin-streamers, combines grace with strength in its proportions and merits high place among the towers of the West of England. Note its loftiness by comparison with the typically Devonian, low, unclerestoried nave. Sometimes Decorated windows from the former church were built into the new tower. Examples of this are to be found at Moretonhampstead—a four-stage tower under construction in 1418—Chagford, Drewsteignton, Buckland-in-the-Moor, and Bickington.

There are numerous examples in the county of the wagon or cradle roof of this period. The distinguishing feature is the curved ribs to the simple collared rafter, with every fourth rib projecting a moulding within the general concave surface. The absence of the chancel arch results in a continuous roof, without break between chancel and nave. In many roofs, the spaces between the moulded members are plastered and there has been some controversy as to whether this was the original medieval practice or, as is generally believed, the plastering was done in the course of subsequent restorations.

Frequently, as at Kentisbeare, Holcombe Rogus, Rewe, Chulmleigh and Lapford, carved angels are planted against the wallplate in front of the springing of the main rib, standing on a timber end projecting from the wall below. That of Abbotsham rests on wooden figures holding painted shields with emblems of various trades—a gardener's spade, hoe and rake, a carpenter's square, hammer and axe, and a mason's trowel. Roof bosses that cover the mitering together of the moulded main arched ribs with the three or four longitudinal ones vary greatly in character; some are spiritedly carved, while others are tame and uncouth. Chulmleigh, with ceiling wagon-roofs throughout carrying 180 bosses and thirty-eight carved angels, is a particularly good example of Devon's Perpendicular roofing. Nearby, Chawleigh boasts 120 bosses, and there is another noteworthy series of carved bosses at Dunchideock, among them a remarkable number of heads. Some are grotesque: crescent moon, elaborate knots, pig's head, Turk's head, three fishes with their tails in each other's mouths (the latter a symbol of eternity).

At Harberton, the long wagon roofs are aglow with painted beams and golden bosses, lit up with colour as our churches were meant to be. The eighty different carved bosses are mostly decorative, though some represent legendary figures. The nave here has been claimed as *c* 1370, but it was not until 1436 that Bishop Lacy granted 'forty days indulgence to all contributing to the reparation and building of the parish church of Harberton', so that it is to this date that the roofs must be attributed.

Hartland, too, is a church full of colour—especially in the eastern parts where there are some beautifully-painted stars in the panels. At Winkleigh there are seventy golden-winged angels on the wall-plates, and every beam and boss is gaily painted. The ceiled chancel roof of Payhembury—square panels with diagonal ribs—competes with the roodscreen for beauty of colour, also vividly exemplified in Devon's eight celures, or canopies of honour. The Reverend Charles Scriven, writing

Hennock: the celure is in its original colouring of blue and gold, and is one of the few to survive

in the 1869 *Transactions of Exeter Diocesan Architectural Society* Vol 3, declares that all churches in the district around Exeter formerly had celures over the head of the great rood. And perhaps the best of them all is that at Hennock, decorated in its original colouring of blue and gold, with suns and stars.

But if Hennock can claim pride of place in celures, then surely the finest cradle roof in Devon covers the nave and chancel of Cullompton. Every rib of the squares and the diagonals is feathered with a leaf cresting, the red, blue and gold of the roof providing a vivid backcloth for all this splendour. And, strikingly in contrast to such strength and richness, is the delicate fan vaulting above the south aisle, the chantry of John Lane, inspired by the Dorset aisle of 1520 at Ottery St Mary. It was fortunate indeed that such exquisite work escaped the great fire of 1839 which destroyed the greater part of the town.

Whilst arcades are surprisingly uniform—whether of Beer stone, granite, or red sandstone—the lovely 'Devon wreathing' of the Beer stone capitals is found to perfection in the country churches, usually in the form of a horizontal frieze of carved foliage. Perhaps the finest example is at Bradninch where the wreathing adorns the graceful piers, though Stoke-in-Teignhead has the best display of figure sculpture, and at Ottery St Mary particularly fine craftsmanship is displayed in the foliage, the grotesques, particularly the elephant's head, and in the ribbon work of the Dorset aisle pier capitals. In the early fifteenth-century work at Crediton, where the height of the massive piers was limited by the retention of the old crossing arches, the angle shafts alone have capitals. The sides of the piers are moulded in broad waves, and these are continued without a break through the arches, with a course in Beer stone at the level of the capitals of the shafts. This arrangement can also be seen at Little Hempston and Atherington.

Evidence of date may sometimes be ascertained

Cullompton :
Devon's finest wagon roof.
The inspiration no doubt came from
Shepton Mallet (Somerset)

from these pier caps, for some have shields of heraldic arms carved upon them—often an impalement of marriage, such as that at Powderham where Courtenay impales Bonville, a marriage which is known to have taken place between 1485 and 1487. At Coffinswell, there are four shields illustrating four different marriages of the Holbeam family, lords of the manor who lived at Holbeam, while Payhembury is fortunate in the possession of capitals bearing the well-carved arms of the Bourchier, Courtenay, Ferrers and Malherbe families. Again, too, the rose of Edward IV which adorns Tiverton, St Peter, affords a clue to its date.

Perpendicular Devon windows are relatively uniform, though not as standardized as piers. The finest examples are the three west windows of Colyton, the side ones having four lights, and the central one nine, with two transoms. Measuring 19 by 30 ft, this is one of the largest west windows to be seen in any English parish church, and may well owe its existence to the fact that, thanks to the cloth trade, Colyton was at the time one of the three wealthiest towns in the county. Other notable windows are those of the Dorset and Lane aisles at Ottery St Mary and Cullompton, those of Torbryan, and the eight-light west window of Crediton. The church at Crediton was almost in ruins in the first decade of the fifteenth century, but when rebuilding did start in 1413, it continued for over thirty years. As at the other cloth towns, Crediton wealth found an outlet in church architecture; the roofs were raised and more light was let in by the use of the clerestory—three-light windows in the nave, four-light in the chancel. Those windows, now as then, are the glory of Crediton, the ones in the aisles and transepts being particularly well proportioned.

The five large fifteenth-century windows of Doddiscombsleigh's north aisle preserve their

Stoke-in-Teignhead : figure-sculpture in Beer stone. Shield-holding angels with saints between them

original glass almost intact. For this, Devon can be particularly thankful as it is peculiarly ill-served in the preservation of ancient stained glass. Apart from four windows in Exeter Cathedral, the Doddiscombsleigh ones are the only complete windows in the county to have survived. The east window showing the seven sacraments is of exceptional interest. At Ashton, in the three eastern-most windows of the north aisle, a fine series of heraldic shields display the impalements of the Chudleigh family, whose connection with the parish began early in the fourteenth century and lasted for 400 years. F. Morris Drake in *The Archaeological Journal* of 1913 claims that the glass here is by a French painter and even better than that at Doddiscombsleigh.

An essential part of most rebuildings was the provision of south porches, some of great beauty, and many of them two-storeyed and embattled. Pride of place here must surely go to Kenton, whose porch is complete with parvise chamber and the finest Perpendicular doorway in the diocese. The porch, with three image niches above the door, incorporates the corbelled heads of Henry IV and Joan of Navarre, and though the vaulting has disappeared, the whole church is an admirable example of its period. Other south porches, less imposing in design but still retaining excellent vaulting and carved bosses, include Berry Pomeroy and Marldon.

Kenton, incidentally, has long been the subject of controversy concerning its date. Cresswell and Pevsner, like others before them, have been 'led

Exeter, St Martin :
the best known of Exeter's
small churches. Dedicated, 1065.
Perpendicular window, 1417

astray' by the will of William Slighe, dated 1379, in which he expresses a desire to be buried in the aisle of the parish church which he had newly erected. As with Dittisham (1337), *de novo constructum* implies repair and enlargement work which was swept away during the Tudor reconstruction. Thompson suggests 'not earlier than the reign of Henry VII' for Kenton, while Rickman's *Gothic Architecture* dates it all as *c* 1500. The pier arcades are of the same type as those of nearby Powderham.

The most sumptuous displays of Perpendicular architecture in the county are undoubtedly the Greenway aisle at Tiverton, the Lane aisle at Cullompton, and the Dorset aisle at Ottery St Mary —three instances of private wealth lavished upon the focal point of life in the medieval community. Before examining the real effect of this wealth, we can summarise as follows:

1. PERPENDICULAR GOTHIC:

    Finest examples: Ashburton, Broadclyst, Broadhembury, Buckland Monachorum (entirely of granite), Chittlehampton, Crediton, Cullompton, Harberton, Hartland, Kenton, Kingsteignton, North Molton, Ottery St Mary (Dorset aisle), Paignton, Plymouth, St Andrew; Plympton St Mary, Sampford Courtenay, South Molton, Tavistock, Tiverton, St Peter; Torbryan, Totnes, Widecombe-in-the-Moor.

2. Other good examples: Atherington, Ashton, Berry Pomeroy, Berrynarbor, Bishops Nympton, Bradninch, Combe Martin, Chagford, Holcombe Rogus, Ilsington, Ipplepen, Kentisbeare, Marldon, Payhembury, Plymtree, Silverton, Stokenham, Talaton, Upton Pyne, West Alvington, Winkleigh.

3. BUILDING IN CHRONOLOGICAL ORDER, where evidence of date is available. As building generally spanned several years, the period is divided into sixteen decades.

1390s Bradworthy, Buckland Brewer, Cheriton Bishop (tower), Coldridge, Poltimore, Whitestone.

1400s Broadhempston, Buckerell, Dartmouth, St Saviour (chancel); Lympstone, Upton Hellions, Woodbury.

1410s Bow (north aisle), Broadclyst, Bulkworthy, Combe Martin, Crediton, Down St Mary, Eggesford, Exeter, St Thomas; Honiton, St Michael; Moretonhampstead, Newton St Cyres, Nymet Rowland.

1420s Ashton, Hartland (tower), Highweek, Monkleigh, Ugborough.

1430s Ashburton, Bradninch, Brixham, St Mary; Buckland Brewer, Dartmouth, St Petrock; Dawlish, Dunsford, Exeter, St Martin; Gittisham (south aisle), Harberton, Huntshaw, Ilfracombe, Landcross, Lapford, Little Torrington, Paignton, Satterleigh, South Molton, Stokenham, Tavistock, Teigngrace (rebuilt 1787), Totnes (nave).

1440s Ashburton, Coffinswell, East Budleigh, Ipplepen, Okehampton (all but tower destroyed by fire 1842), Plymouth, St Andrew (burnt out in air raids; restored since the war); Salcombe Regis (tower), Sidbury, Swimbridge, Tavistock, Torbryan, Totnes (chancel).

1450s Bickleigh, near Plymouth (tower); Bishops Tawton (north aisle), Marldon, Morchard Bishop, North Molton, Spreyton, Totnes (tower).

1460s Branscombe (east window), Colebrooke (north chancel aisle), Honiton, St Michael (tower); Plymouth, St Andrew (tower).

1470s Hennock, Little Hempston (for long misdated 1439).

1480s Axminster (south chancel aisle), Berrynarbor (tower), Berry Pomeroy, Bovey Tracey, Chittlehampton, Ilsington, Powderham, Silverton (north aisle), Swimbridge (transept), Tiverton, St Peter

1490s Broadclyst (except tower), Cockington, Manaton, Sampford Peverell (south aisle), Shillingford.

1500s Berrynarbor, Hittisleigh (north aisle), Holcombe Rogus (north aisle), Holne (aisles), Holsworthy (tower), Kenton, North Molton (clerestory), Romansleigh, Uplowman, Welcombe, Westleigh (aisles).

1510s Coldridge, Mary Tavy (tower), Wolborough (tower).

1520s Cruwys Morchard (south aisle), Cullompton (Lane aisle), Honiton, St Michael (aisles); Kentisbeare (south aisle), Littleham, near Exmouth (north aisle); Marldon (south chancel aisle), Ottery St Mary (Dorset aisle), Thornbury, Tiverton, St Peter (tower and Greenway chapel); Ugborough (tower).

1530s Bradford (north aisle), Broadclyst (tower), Christow, Widecombe-in-the-Moor (tower), Woodland.

1540s Cullompton (tower), Heavitree (rebuilt nineteenth century), Horwood, Instow (north aisle), Mortehoe, Plympton, St Maurice; Tawstock (chancel aisle), Totnes (north aisle).

MEDIEVAL WEALTH

The building of churches represented an obvious means by which the wealthy could offer substance to God in a period when organised philanthropy, as we know it, was virtually unknown and the endowment of schools or almshouses still very much in its infancy. So it was that the Church in Devon owed much to its devout men of business, the merchant princes of 'an age of wool' and, to a lesser extent, the mineral prospectors who had found riches in places such as Combe Martin, North Molton, and upon Dartmoor. Prosperity in the wool trade reached its peak at the end of this period,

Tavistock, St Eustace : fifteenth century.
A large church, enriched by the local cloth trade

64

and the tin trade, which showed a steady upward trend from 1450 to 1530, had hundreds of shareholders throughout the county, from the Lord Bishop and the Earl of Devon downwards. Moreover, the county as a whole was happily immune from any effects of the depression which overshadowed a great part of England at the time.

Thus, as in Norfolk and Suffolk, the growing wealth of lay-folk generally provided means for the development of church architecture in Devon on a more elaborate scale than ever before. Money for furnishings and contributions towards church upkeep came from all but the labouring classes, with particularly handsome donations towards the cost of extending and beautifying their parish church from those among the landed gentry and successful lawyers who were beginning to suspect that their worldly prosperity was not entirely of

their own making. And rare indeed was the medieval will that did not contain a bequest of one sort or another to the Church.

The entire reconstruction of St Clement's, Powderham, in the early 1480s obviously owed much to the generosity of the Courtenays, an ancient and influential family long before Powderham came into their possession. Though, unusually, the church lacks memorials to the family—other than their arms on the pier capitals at the east end —we learn from the will of Margaret, Lady Courtenay (1487) of her desire to be buried—

'nigh to my late husband in Powderham church, for my husband and I made there the new ile and also the body of the church at our owne coste and charge except that I had of the parish to the help of the said building VIIId'.

At Holcombe Rogus, the lordship of the manor

Doddiscombsleigh: medieval glass. An example of wealth in the form of fifteenth-century stained glass was held by the Bluett family from the time of Henry VII, and it was they who built the north aisle, with its remarkable open cradle roof. The church still holds many interesting monuments to the family, and the Bluett pew is a rare example of a completely preserved Jacobean family pew.

Bulkworthy, tiny, picturesque, and most unusual with its bellcote (of 1873), was founded in the year after Henry V's coronation by Sir William Hankford, Chief Justice of the King's Bench, who lived at Annery. He was also associated with the rebuilding of the fabric at nearby Monkleigh nine years later, and left money in his will for completion and maintenance of the south aisle on condition that he and his heirs should have a burial place there. This is the Annery chapel, in which there is a monument to this great lawyer benefactor.

Marldon, with castellated north and south aisles, was built almost entirely by a fifteenth-century sheriff of Devon, Otho Gilbert, of Compton Castle, and his wife Elizabeth. Later, in the 1520s, John Gilbert—who transformed his small manor house into a spectacular fortress—built the south chancel aisle known as the Compton chapel. His coat of arms appears on the east respond, and again on the bosses in the vaulted porch.

The Copleston chantry chapel, or aisle, at Colebrooke—with an oddly flamboyant window, quite untypical of Devon—was built about 1460 by Philip Copleston. The chantry was founded by his younger brother Walter, in memory of their father. The two bench-ends, or priedieux, now in the chancel, were originally in this chapel and feature the arms of Copleston and Gorges, borne by grotesque men. They were probably carved in 1472, the year in which these two families were joined by marriage. The chapel originally possessed a fireplace with a chimney dating from the second half of the sixteenth century, but this has since been blocked up, though the stone chimney can still be seen on the outside wall. The earlier south transept, or Horwell aisle as it is called from the estate with which it goes, was built by Sir Walter de Bathe, lord of the manor in the early fourteenth century. The Gilberts and the Coplestons still maintain a close connection with their ancestral churches.

Sir William Huddersfield built the tower of Shillingford, on to what was the small domestic chapel of the Shillingford family. It incorporates the arms of its builder and his wife, Katherine Courtenay. In the chancel is the tomb-chest and monumental brass to these benefactors and their three children. At Silverton, John Swyfmore, a one-time rector, directed in his will dated 18 June 1478 that his body was to be buried before the image of the Virgin Mary. He left forty pounds for the erection of a new aisle and bequeathed all his lands and tenements in Silverton for the support of a priest to sing masses for him in the church. The north aisle was duly built a few years after his

Bovey Tracey: pulpit and roodscreen. Magnificent examples of medieval craftsmanship. The gift of Lady Margaret Beaufort

death. Swyforme's bequest was by no means uncommon and clerics, no less than laymen, made their contributions towards the extensive rebuilding then in progress.

At Crediton, in 1411, Ralph Tregrisiow, dean of Exeter, left one hundred shillings towards rebuilding the Church of the Holy Cross. William Langeton, one of the canons and prebendaries, willed the surplus revenues of his prebend, while Canon Richard Penelz donated the sum of twenty pounds. Thomas Barton, canon of Exeter and Crediton, and rector of Ilfracombe, also left twenty pounds for the construction of a new window, the raising of the walls, and timber for the roof of the north transept, so that it might be completed to match the other. His bequest was conditional upon the other canons or parishioners contributing the same amount, failing which his bequest was to go to the high altar and stone screens for the presbytery, with two small tablets of alabaster, 'honestly painted', for the little altars in the choir aisles.

The chancel wagon roof of Spreyton bears the name of Henry le Maygne. He was the incumbent in 1451, 'a native of Normandy who caused me to be built', and who, 'wrote all this with his own hand'. Also recorded there are the names of Robert of Becdenne, Prior of Cowick, and Richard Talbot, Lord of Spreyton, who 'gave all their goods to my building'. An ashlar-built granite church, Spreyton is typically Cornish in appearance.

Buried beneath the church of Axminster are several members of the Yonge family, who added the south chancel aisle to St Mary's in about 1480. Their mansion house, where they lived from 1450 to 1700, stood on the eastern side of the market place. The same year, 1480, also saw the rebuilding of Berry Pomeroy (north and south aisles embattled), where the capitals of the south arcade bear the names of parishioners—seven men and their wives—who contributed to its cost. The north

Exeter, St Mary Steps: medieval clock. The famous Matthew the Miller clock. Early sixteenth century

aisle and south porch are said to have been built by Sir Richard Pomeroy, who is buried at the north side of the altar.

Lady Margaret Beaufort, Countess of Richmond and Derby, and Henry VII's mother, owned several estates in Devon, and much of the reconstruction of Bovey Tracey (arcades similar to Powderham and Kenton) and its beautiful furnishings—rood-screen, pulpit, lectern, misericordia and font—are due to her generosity. In 1498, at Sampford Peverell, she also financed construction of the south aisle, with its decorated west gable, quatrefoil panelling and three-light windows. Two years later, at nearby Uplowman, she was responsible for building a completely new church, which was largely rebuilt in 1864.

The owners of Thuborough House in Sutcombe —first De Esse, then Giffard, and later Prideaux— rebuilt, extended and enriched this sanctuary throughout the fifteenth and sixteenth centuries.

Stephen Giffard, who died in 1475, was probably responsible for the Thuborough aisle, or south chapel. It was completed by the glazing of the east window, whose coats of arms indicate a date somewhere between 1443 and 1475. The north aisle, extending the whole length of the building, was added shortly afterwards. The capitals of the five-bay granite pier-arcade, c 1480, show the Prideaux arms and those of families related by marriage. At Lapford, the manor came to the St John family in about 1430, and to them may be attributed the substantial rebuilding of the church. Among its remarkable bench-ends are several bearing the initials and monograms of the new lords.

Much of the glory of Honiton, St Michael, was destroyed by the disastrous fire of 1911, but enough remains to show the extent of its debt to Bishop Peter Courtenay of Exeter and John and Joan Takell. Bishop Courtenay, who was also lord of the manor, built and paid for the tower and was a major con-

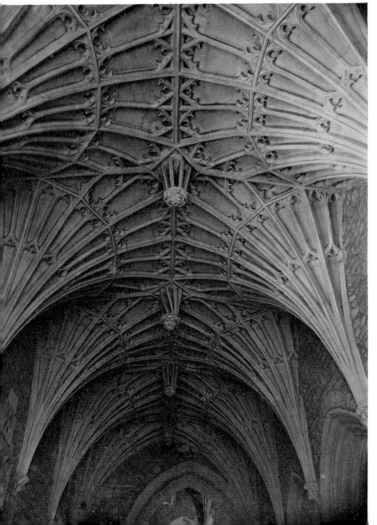

Ottery St Mary: Dorset aisle vaulting.
The remarkable fan-vaulting, c 1520

tributor to the cost of erecting the cruciform-plan church itself. Later, north and south nave and chancel aisles, the arcades, and the south porch, with its beautiful doorway carved with grapes and vines, were added by John Takell, a wealthy Tudor merchant and a burgess of Honiton. It was also through his generosity and that of his wife that the roodscreen (46 ft long and of the 'Exe Valley' type) was erected about 1525. The present screen is an exact copy of the original.

Sir John Evans, described as park-keeper to Henry VIII, was responsible for the renovation of the fabric of Coldridge, and for many of the fittings, including bench-ends, pulpit, parclose and rood-screen, all c 1511. Nave and aisles were reconstructed with three-light windows of various but not unusual Perpendicular tracery pattern. The flamboyant tracery of the parclose screen separates the chancel from Sir John's chantry chapel, within which can be seen his effigy in armour. At Plymouth

Thomas Yogge, a prosperous merchant and three times mayor of the town, bore the cost of the granite tower of St Andrew's (at this date, 1460, its only church) on condition that the townsfolk should provide 'the stuffe', or the materials. At Kentisbeare, a merchant, John Whytyng, built the south aisle which now contains his altar-tomb, and probably also gave the roodscreen which bears his arms. A woolpack and a Tudor ship on the heraldic shield of the Merchant Adventurers of London can also be seen on one of the capitals of the south arcade.

The south aisle of Gittisham was built by Henry Beaumont and, again, his arms are on the capitals. The north aisle of Littleham, near Exmouth, with straight-headed four-light windows, was added by the Drake family in 1528. At Instow, the north aisle, with straight-headed three-light windows and ceiled wagon roof, was added in 1547, and an unusual inscription around the capitals tells how

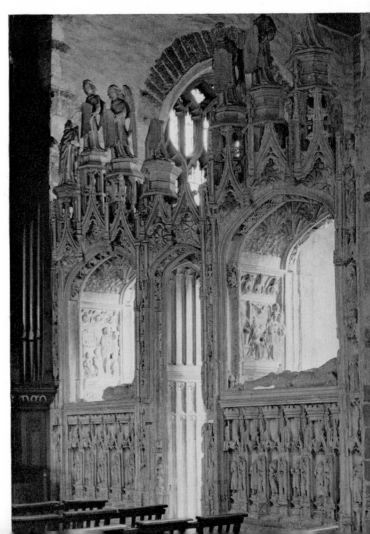

Paignton: Kirkham chantry. Erected in the south transept by the Kirkhams of Blagdon. Late fifteenth century

it was built by Rycharde Waterman and Emma his wife. The aisles of Parkham were built, on the north, by the Risdons of Bableigh, and on the south by the Giffards of Halsbury. The capitals of the granite arcade between the nave and south aisle are carved with initial letters. At Shebbear, the south aisle was the gift of Lady Prendergast of Ladford. Her recumbent figure, with rosary, and angels holding up her cushioned head, is in the south wall. The north aisle of Ashcombe was added by the Kirkhams, lords of the manor, and their arms may be seen on the arcade capitals and on one of the bench-ends. The Ayshford family built their own aisle at Burlescombe, and the church contains their monuments, as well as depicting their arms on the Beer-stone capitals.

Benefactors of yet other aisles in Devon churches included John Pollard and his wife Emma, who built the Pollard aisle of Horwood, and John Bourchier, second Earl of Bath, who built the south chancel aisle of Tawstock, with its rich cradle roof. The Dorset aisle of Ottery St Mary, with its remarkable fan-vaulted roof and five large pendant bosses of open tracery terminating in Tudor roses, was given by the heiress, Cecily Bonville, who was at the same time Countess of Wiltshire and Huntingdon, Marchioness of Dorset, and several times a baroness.

Other notable family benefactors were the Bampfyldes (later to become the Lords Poltimore) at North Molton and Poltimore, the Chudleighs at Broadclyst, the Furlongs and the Wises at Loddiswell, the Champernownes of Modbury, the Kellys of Kelly—and so one could go on from the Atlantic to Lyme Bay and from the Bristol Channel to Plymouth Sound. Many of these monuments to family splendour endure but outstanding among them all must surely be the late fifteenth-century screen and monuments of the Kirkham family, occupying the south transept at Paignton, which was later converted into a chantry chapel. The stone screen, Tudor-arched with figure sculpture and ornament, though barbarously mutilated, is still beautiful.

The first quarter of the sixteenth century was perhaps the heyday of Devon's merchant princes

Tiverton, St Peter : John Greenway's chapel and south porch of 1517. A real showpiece

and to two of them in particular, John Greenway of Tiverton and John Lane of Cullompton, we are indebted for some notable examples of the architectural magnificence of that period. The minute realism of the carvings of Greenway's chapel and south porch (1517) gives them a high place among the works of Gothic art in England. The whole of the south side was rebuilt by him, and is lavishly carved with all manner of decoration including ships, wool-packs, staple-marks, coats of arms, and figures of men, children and horses. The frieze of ships depicts the armed merchantmen or galliasses of the period, in which Greenway and other members of the Merchant Adventurers' Company transported their goods. On the corbel line, which runs round the whole of the chapel, twenty-one of the principal events in the life of Our Lord are represented in relief, beginning with the flight into Egypt and ending with the Ascension.

The building of the Lane aisle at Cullompton began in 1526, but its benefactor never saw the full nobility of the work his wealth had bought, for he died in 1528. Construction of the aisle continued for several years afterwards, and was possibly completed in 1549, at the same time as the tower. There are five windows of four lights on the south side, a similar window to the east, and a six-light window to the west. Between the windows are buttresses carved with merchants' marks and other devices, four of the carvings representing ships in minute detail. The interior has a remarkable stone fan-vaulted roof in which the twelve compartments spring from angel corbels. Amidst these treasures, John Lane and his wife lie buried, but their brasses, unfortunately, have been removed.

As A. K. Wickham says in the introduction to his *Churches of Somerset*, 1965, 'Perpendicular architecture is now generally regarded as the perfect consummation of the Gothic style in this country, and one of the greatest English contributions to art'. Yet few of us realise how very much of it was owed to private fortunes and the benefaction of wealthy families.

Cullompton : Lane aisle. The gift of merchant John Lane, 1526. Stone fan-vaulted roof of twelve compartments

7. Building Stone

Nowhere are stronger local characteristics in parish church-building to be found than in the Perpendicular churches of the West of England. This is largely because each area drew upon building material that was readily to hand and such was the variety of material that each locality possesses its own distinctive peculiarities of architecture. Devon, in particular, with its complex geology, provides a remarkable range of serviceable building stone—so much so, indeed, that a geological map is an almost essential aid to the full appreciation of Devonshire churches. No small part of the great beauty of the county's medieval village churches lies in the colour of their stone, a beauty accentuated by the spreading branches of many fine churchyard yews, lichens and mosses, the colour-

Totnes : apart from its broad red tower,
the roodscreen, of Beer stone, is the pride of Totnes

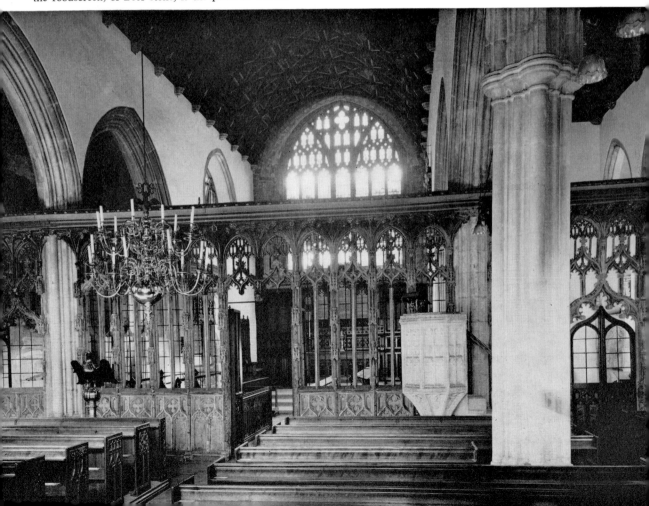

washed cob of nearby cottages and the golden glow of their thatch, and the lush green of well-watered pastures.

The county possesses three distinct main types of building stone. These are the New Red Sandstone which runs from west of Bridgwater in Somerset down to the sea at Torbay; the cream-coloured stone of Beer, a chalk-rock of south-east Devon used principally for interior work; and the dark grey granite of the Dartmoor region, supplemented in the north by granite from Lundy. Flint and limestone are seen only when there were quarries in the immediate vicinity, while Ham Hill (Somerset) stone—as we have already seen at Tawstock—was favoured for window tracery, and

also for arches in certain areas in north and east Devon. It is only later, as means of transport improved and the industrial revolution gained momentum, that we notice the introduction of building materials quite foreign to the county.

Decoration is seen to be at its richest where the Red Sandstone and Beer stone are combined, as is frequently the case in east Devon. Granite churches are less ornate, decorations upon the capitals and piers are frequently shallow and poor; indeed, the building is often so severe in style as to give the impression of being of earlier origin than it really is. Yet much of this apparent conservatism was, in fact, dictated by the difficulty of getting really good freestone at an economic price. Parishes in the

Kenton : of red sandstone.
Fully developed
Perpendicular of *c* 1500

south-east were fortunate in having near access to Beer stone, but for others it had to be brought some distance and was correspondingly costly. Limestone was abundant in many parts, but could only be used for rubble walling. Schist was only a trifle better and, apart from rubble walling, could only be employed for the plinth and battlement, and suchlike members where only a chamfer or a splay had to be wrought. Red Sandstone, though plentiful, was mostly of the rough conglomerate type, full of large hard nodules and quite incapable of being wrought fine. The carboniferous rock of north Devon was not much better than the limestone of the south.

All this meant that, in spite of the variety of available stone, the majority of doorways and windows had their jambs worked with nothing better than a chamfer. If a superior result was desired the mouldings had to be such as not to require deep sinking; hence we find such mouldings as a chamfered square recess, a quarter circle with fillets, and several other combinations. For this reason, too, the upper windows of many towers have plain arched heads, without cusps or tracery, resembling Early English or Norman work.

Beer stone was used extensively for interior work in nearly every church in the south-east and also those parts of south Devon which could be reached

Pinhoe : typical of the Exe valley. Local red sandstone. Contains much of interest

by water. It was employed mainly for arcades, and for capitals which were deeply carved. Many piers and capitals are so similar that possibly they were shop-wrought, perhaps at Exeter, or close by. Where no expense was spared—as at Ashton, Doddiscombsleigh and Berrynarbor—wealthy benefactors must have been responsible for defraying the high cost of bringing the stone by sea around the coast. Fine examples of its use are to be seen at Cullompton (also Ham Hill stone); Dartington (nineteenth century); Kingsteignton; South Molton; Torbryan; Wolborough.

At Ermington, Beer stone is used, together with stone from Doulting and Ham Hill in Somerset. At Kentisbeare, a striking effect is achieved by using it in the quoins and buttresses of the tower,

Combe Martin: of local sandstone.
Chancel and south transept, 1250; remainder, 1410

together with Red Sandstone from Upton, near Cullompton. The arcades of Kingskerswell are particularly interesting, being of different stone and different periods. The north is of Beer stone with standard Devon capitals and moulded arches (early fifteenth century), the south of Red Sandstone octagonal piers with red double-chamfered arches and limestone moulded capitals (early sixteenth century).

The broad belt of New Red Sandstone running down to Torbay has contributed to many churches in this region, including that from Dainton, near Newton Abbot, for the early fourteenth-century reconstruction of Haccombe. Later, during the Perpendicular reconstruction, it was usual to employ the harder and rougher local sandstone for the outer walls of churches, in which much of the old materials could be used. Occasionally, instead of complete reconstruction of the arcades, builders short of funds heightened the existing columns and rebuilt the arches upon them. This can be seen at Ipplepen and Paignton. At Halberton, only the three eastern bays were heightened, to provide room for the screen and loft which crosses the whole width in the second bay. The same reconstruction can be seen at Dartmouth, St Saviour.

Good examples of sandstone churches are to be found at Kenton and Pinhoe, and others can be seen all through the valley of the lower Exe, their red towers peeping from between green trees, their colour merging with a landscape of 'redland' soil. At Cullompton and Totnes, only the towers are of sandstone, while at Tiverton, St Peter, only the chancel is sandstone, the remainder being of grey limestone. To the west of Whitestone, towers are of granite but at Whitestone itself there is the interesting combination of granite piers and red sandstone arches. On the north coast, the churches of Berrynarbor and Combe Martin are built of a sandstone quarried locally.

On the edge of this sandstone country in the east, close to the Dorset border, extensive use is made of flint from the green land of the Blackdown. Typical of this use are the churches at Axminster, Colyton, Combe Raleigh, Cotleigh and Southleigh. Flint was also used in the Victorian rebuilding of Rousdon.

On the coast at Salcombe Regis, the greensand quarry of Dunscombe was drawn upon for building the parish church, from c 1152 until the tower was completed in 1445. It also contributed to the restoration of Sidbury in the same year, and probably to the building of the cathedral at Exeter from an even earlier date. In the 1930s, it was reopened for the building of Woolbrook (Sidmouth).

Dressed granite was used in the fourteenth century for quoins or buttresses, but not until the fifteenth century in window tracery and arcades. The excessive labour involved in working it prohibited its use for deep mouldings, cusps, raised members, foliage, etc, though an exception is to be seen in the granite carving on the Cornish church of Launceston. It was seldom that people had both the funds and the patience to execute such work, and even when more elaborate ornament was sometimes attempted, as on the Norman font at Spreyton and the sixteenth-century font of Broadwoodkelly, the carving is so crude as to appear archaic.

Granite piers are generally octagonal monoliths with roughly chamfered bases and spreading capitals. The capitals, usually long and chamfered down irregularly to the top of the shaft, are all of one piece with the apparent abacus, a bead being left above the chamfer without any attempt at undercutting. The arches are simply chamfered, or the chamfer is cut into a shallow hollow or a rudimentary ogee. In other cases, such as at Manaton, the piers have attached shafts at the angles, the sides are scooped into hollows, the capitals have bands of sharp edges or small fillets in imitation of mouldings, and are spread so as to be continuous. The arches have either chamfers or rough ogees. Here and there, as at Spreyton, the piers consist of a cluster of four attached shafts with capitals.

In the South Hams, near Plymouth, and to the west and north of Dartmoor, granite is almost universal. Apart from the all-granite edifice of Buckland Monachorum, there are fine examples at Exbourne, Gidleigh and Spreyton. Indeed, granite is found from Sutcombe in the north (arcades), twenty miles from its nearest source at Okehampton, to Chivelstone (used with local slate) the most southerly parish in the county; from Christow in the east, westward to the Tamar, and beyond into Cornwall. Notable examples of its use are Bovey Tracey (granite window mullions and walls of granite roughcast), Lydford, Manaton, Plympton St Mary, Sampford Courtenay, Shaugh Prior, South Tawton, Throwleigh, Ugborough and Walkhampton. At Sheepstor and Whitchurch, it is used in conjunction with the more tractable Roborough stone, which was a favourite stone in this part for dressings and carved work from the early fourteenth century onwards.

There are splendid granite arcades at Ashburton and Ashwater, Bridford and Burrington. At Broadwoodwidger they are complete with boldly-cut granite capitals, but at Cornworthy the capitals

76

and arches are of limestone. Sampford Courtenay, although principally of granite, incorporates Polyphant stone from Cornwall in its south arcade, and this stone can also be found at Bratton Clovelly. Halwell, mainly of granite, was built in 1879 on to the old west tower of local slate. The earlier, medieval church was no doubt built wholly of slate. In the north, arcades of Lundy granite can be seen at Alwington, Clovelly, Parkham, Woolsery and Yarnscombe, and granite was also used for the piers of Monkleigh.

In addition to the previously mentioned towers of Ashburton, Plymouth, St Andrew, and Widecombe-in-the-Moor, Cheriton Bishop and Holsworthy also have noble medieval towers of granite. Among others, Christow's fine tower, rebuilt in 1630, has its face buttresses set back from the angles and is without a turret, as at Berry Pomeroy and Chagford. Moretonhampstead's tower and arcades are particularly handsome—'Granite Gothic at its finest, almost megalithic', says Hoskins. Milton Abbot and Tavistock show the attractive green stone of Hurdwick—a loose textured, free-working trappean ash quarried on the western fringe of Dartmoor—to best advantage. This stone was extensively used for local building during the nineteenth century.

Finely-bedded slate found west of Dartmouth was used for church-building all over the district from the thirteenth century onwards, and can be seen in the square tower of Dartmouth Castle, built in 1448. The best known quarry was at Charleton, near Kingsbridge. Sherford's church is built entirely of this slate, even to the arcade piers and capitals. It can also be seen at Churchstow,

Sheepstor : fifteenth-century
granite amid the granite rocks of Dartmoor

Dittisham, South Milton and Thurlestone, and the towers of South Pool and Stokenham are particularly fine examples of its use.

In mid-Devon, where a greater variety of building material was used, stone from the ancient Thorverton quarries at Raddon was employed from the twelfth century onwards and can be seen in the arcades and choir of Crediton, at Netherexe, Shobrooke, Upton Hellions, and at several other places in the neighbourhood. To the north, we find a local brown dunstone, as at Bondleigh, West Worlington, and Witheridge. At Newton Tracey, Ham Hill stone was freely used in the construction of the arches, and its procurement is a tribute to the determination of the builders to secure the material they wanted, since its transport must have involved considerable difficulty and expense.

It was probably sea-borne from Bridport around Cornwall to Bideford, or it may have gone down the Somerset waterways to Bridgwater, and so along the coast to Bideford. Stone from Ham Hill can again be seen in the fourteenth-century piers and arcading of Ilfracombe, where it is used with occasional blocks of local blue limestone. It was also used at Bishop's Tawton for the spire and parapet of the tower, and at Axminster (c 1525), on the parapet of the north side.

The Culm Measures of mid-Devon are characterised chiefly by small plain churches built of a chocolate-coloured sandstone. In the poorest parishes, the absence of any building stone that could be carved led to the use of massive oaken arcades, as at Nymet Rowland and Dowland. The remarkable oak arcade of Dowland, c 1500, replaced

Ashburton : of granite, 1430, the tower is the most imposing feature of this fine edifice

an older one, while at Loxhore the north arcade is carried on two fifteenth-century oak piers.

Two good examples in north Devon of building stone which cannot be excelled for strength are the buff limestone arcade piers of the Decorated period to be seen at Hartland, and the Pickwell Down sandstone used in the Perpendicular tower of North Molton. This sandstone came from an old quarry at Flitton close by. In the Exmoor border country, many churches were built of a dark, slaty stone, and the fifteenth-century tower of Kentisbury is a good example of the effective use of this material.

MEDIEVAL QUARRIES
Barley, Budlake (near Killerton), Dunchideock, Heazille (near Rewe), Pocombe, Posbury, Raddon, Silverton—Trap rocks; Posbury stone is red and was used at Crediton and Newton St Cyres.
Beer—Chalk.

Broadclyst, Dainton, Exminster, Galmpton Creek, Heavitree, Kenn, Poltimore, Ugbrooke, Whipton—New Red Sandstone.
Charleton—Slate.
Chudleigh, Ideford, Oreston (near Plymouth)—Limestone.
Cornworthy—Trap rocks or Basalts.
Coryton—Mainly Slates; for roofing, tombstones, etc.
Dunscombe (near Salcombe Regis)—Greensand.
Flitton (near North Molton)—Sandstone.
Hurdwick (near Tavistock)—Trappean ash.
Ipplepen—Devonian Limestone (red and purple marbles).
Lundy—Granite.
Roborough Down—Elvan.
Woodland—Slate (green and purple).
The sources of Dartmoor granite were surface until recent times.

Challacombe : upon Exmoor;
built of a local slatey stone. Rebuilt 1850, except tower

8. Roodscreens

In the West of England, carving, either in stone or more generally in wood, was the chief form of ornamentation of the Perpendicular period. From very early times there had been some form of screen or division between priest and people, between chancel and nave—the name 'chancel' derives from the *cancelli*, or screens, which separated sanctuary from congregation—and with the increasing adoption of the 'open plan' layout these screens rapidly assumed a new importance. For the sculptor and woodcarver they offered welcome opportunities for the expression of their skill, and our Devon churches owe not a little of their beauty and some of their finest treasures to the superb craftsmanship these men displayed. As the joiner's craft developed, so wooden screenwork matured, eventually to reach the height of its perfection in the late fifteenth century. By then, the accumulated experience of generations of native craftsmen, much of whose work was fostered by the monasteries, had resulted in a mastery of design and executive ability that has never yet been surpassed.

Devon is particularly rich in vaulted screens, its total of rather more than fifty being unapproached by any other county in England. The West Country type of screen is easily recognisable, not only in the character of its detail but to an even greater extent by the general construction of its parts. West Country screens usually consist of a series of rich fenestrations of open compartment divided by moulded and carved standards about 3 ft apart, framed with a sill at floor level and having a transom rail about 3 ft 6 in above. The space between sill and transom is filled with three or four vertical

Marwood: roodscreen.
c 1535. Ribbed coving
with Early Renaissance
motifs between the ribs

Kenton: nineteenth-century reconstruction of medieval pulpit,
roodscreen and roodloft

panels with traceried heads, the plain surfaces below being often covered by painted figures. The arcaded openings above the dado-rail are each again divided into three or four compartments by light shafts, and the arched heads filled with tracery, usually of the regular Perpendicular type. Above the open tracery, and projecting from the spandrils of the arches, is a rich vaulting of polygonal section, with moulded ribs, and panels enriched with single tracery, or carvings in low relief. Whilst the East Anglian screens are known for their height, grace, and lightness, those of Devon are squat, rich in detail and heavy from the weight of so much carved ornament.

Altogether, about 150 examples of screenwork remain, though some are badly mutilated and only partly preserved. The real tragedy is not that so many were destroyed by the Reformers or Oliver Cromwell but that the worst destruction took place in the nineteenth century, when their injudicious removal too often left an empty shell, naked and forlorn. No less than forty-five screens disappeared between 1800 and 1850, nineteen in the second half of the century, and two in the 1900s.

The records make dismal reading. At South Brent, the screen was removed in 1864 and allowed to perish. The one at Broadhembury was removed in 1851 and burnt in a shed. Woodbury's was ruined in 1848 by a modernising vicar who claimed that it prevented his voice from being heard. Bulkworthy's, says the record, was 'mutilated after 1847, removed in 1873'. At Wembury, the rood-screen was destroyed shortly before 1852 by a churchwarden, and that of Shebbear was removed in 1887 at a 'restoration', although an evangelical curate had torn some of it down seventy-five years

Willand: an early type of roodscreen, *c* 1400. Simple tracery gaily painted

Awliscombe: roodscreen of Beer stone,
c 1520. A splendid survival of this work

earlier. Sheepstor's screen was reported in 1910 to have been removed 'in recent years' by the lord of the manor, Sir Massey Lopes, but, fortunately, enough fragments were discovered in 1914 for an exact copy to be reconstructed.

In almost every case, too, the ornamental work which once enclosed the loft on east and west sides has completely disappeared. This was partly in obedience to orders from Elizabeth's archbishops and partly to the wear and tear resulting from their post-Reformation use as music and organ galleries, or even in some instances as pews. Only about twelve original examples remain in the whole of England, and two of these are in Devon at Ather-

ington and Marwood. Both are now reduced to only the north aisle section but enough remains of both screens and lofts to show the choice and delicate carvings with their Renaissance detail. The one at Atherington was the work of John Parrys of Northlew, though Roger Down and John Hyll of Chittlehampton were appointed as 'carpenters, carvers and joiners' to complete it.

Other screens which retain portions of the ornamentation of their roodlofts, canopied niche-work, standards, cornices, and crestings include one at Kenton, where so much remained that it has been possible to effect a genuine restoration. Roodlofts reconstructed on medieval models include those at

Staverton, Lewtrenchard and Littleham, near Bideford. The latter is based on that of Partrishow, in the Black Mountains of the Welsh border and, while differing widely from the local type, is interesting for its faithful adherance to the old-time arrangements. The old screen of Lewtrenchard was removed and broken up in 1833 by the grandfather of the Reverend Sabine Baring Gould who, when a boy, rescued enough of the framework and enrichments from the wood heap to make a reconstruction possible. The added roodloft is similar to Atherington.

No student of West Country screenwork should fail to consult the work of those two great authorities, Frederick Bligh Bond and the Reverend Dom Bede Camm who, over many years, carried out a patient examination of virtually every screen in the county. Their classic work, *Roodscreens and Roodlofts* 2 Vols, 1909, is a masterpiece in the study of ecclesiastical woodcarving.

Whilst Devon screens vary in date from about 1420 (e g Halberton and Uffculme) to 1540 or thereabouts, the great majority were erected between 1470 and 1520, as indicated by the badges of kings, queens and nobles, or the initials of bishops which they carry. There was, however, an earlier type, though only a very small number remain as they were either swept away during the great rebuilding, or removed to make way for the more imposing screens which followed. Examples to be seen at Braunton, Exbourne and Willand exhibit a series of lights, set in a flat rectangular framework under a horizontal beam, above which was a flat or projecting coved soffit under the roodloft. Similar in design but executed in Beer stone is the screen at Awliscombe, which was constructed early in the sixteenth century and is one of the twelve stone screens in the county. Ashburton's, although similar in type, is more modern, having been erected in 1884, by G. E. Street. Those of Brushford, Colebrooke, Monkleigh and West Worlington, though also rectangular, are later works and were never designed for roodlofts. Similar, too, are the post-Reformation screens of Cruwys Morchard, Ermington, Holbeton, Lustleigh and Washford but, again, these never supported lofts. Washfield has a projecting top recalling the earlier type but is here simply an ornamental member.

In addition to the early flat-headed type, Bligh Bond classified the screens of Devon as follows:

1. Ordinary Perpendicular. Found with minor variations all over the county.
2. Enriched Perpendicular. A marked superiority of detail, as at Kenton.
3. Hartland - Burrington type. The lights are divided by a heavy moulded standard running into the apex of the arch, the vaulting spandrels being richly embossed and the cornices very fine.
4. Perpendicular - 'Exe Valley' type. The introduction of miniature shields into the open tracery is a distinguishing feature.
5. Halberton - Uffculme type. Comparatively plain. An early and massive type of Perpendicular.
6. Dartmouth type. A distinctive character of tracery, containing foliated canopies within the arcaded window heads. The vaulting also has a special character.
7. Bridford type. A highly enriched variety of late Perpendicular with a slight admixture of Renaissance feeling.
8. Lapford type. A tracery system of Perpendicular character with cornices chiefly of native design. The fillings of the vaultings and other members exhibit a strong Renaissance admixture.
9. Holbeton type. Hispano - Flemish influence, mainly seen in parclose screens.
10. Colebrook type. French - Moorish influence.
11. Pilton type. Similar to the early vaulted screens but much richer and exhibits a number of florid decorated forms.

The painted screens of Devon, though hardly subscribing to the artistic standards of East Anglian screens, are nonetheless the chief glory of the churches they adorn. It would be difficult now to exaggerate their beauty, but how glorious must they have been when, still intact with carved and painted roodlofts and surmounted by the great rood itself, as now restored at Ashburton, Dartmouth, St Saviour, and Kenn, they stood accompanied, as was the custom of the time, by the figures of the Blessed Virgin Mary and St John Evangelist, glowing with gold and colour and glittering in the light of the wax-tapers and lamps of olive oil which burned continually before the screen. The whole of the intricate and exquisite carving in cornice, breast-summer, cresting, muntins and panels, would have been ablaze with gilding, the saints shining forth resplendent from the panels of the loft above and of the screen below, like a heavenly court surrounding the throne of the Crucified King.

The most artistic paintings are those on the parclose screen at Ashton, surpassing, says Aymer Vallance, any other in the West of England. Of about 1525, they are unlike anything else in Devon

—a well-preserved and finely executed series of prophets, half length, so that there is no impression of their appearing stunted in proportion to the width of the panels they occupy. Another series at Plymtree—one of the most perfect sets—is almost equally beautiful and, except for one bay, the colouring is unrestored. The Sibyls at Bradninch (1528), too, have a grace and charm of their own. Opinions differ as to the quality of the screen paintings to be seen at Buckland-in-the-Moor, but although, like those of Manaton, they are now much defaced, they still show evidence of great skill in execution. The painter of the figures at Ipplepen was a true artist and the hand that drew the little figures at Hennock was not unskilful.

Those of Holne and Kenton are distinguished by their quaintness, while the figures of the Apostles at Sherford are almost good enough to compete with similar works in Norfolk.

Many of Devon's paintings were destroyed or ruined by the nineteenth-century 'restorers', and one in particular, Dr Earle, Dean of Exeter, is notorious for having himself removed or painted over many screens. Among those that remain—and they are all the more precious—there is a curious scarcity of English saints; our medieval forefathers were extremely catholic in their devotional tastes. There are many paintings of the Annunciation (Bovey Tracey, Bradninch); of the Coronation of Mary (Holne, Torbryan, Portle-

Burrington: early sixteenth-century roodscreen.
Eight bays; bears some resemblance to Lapford and Atherington

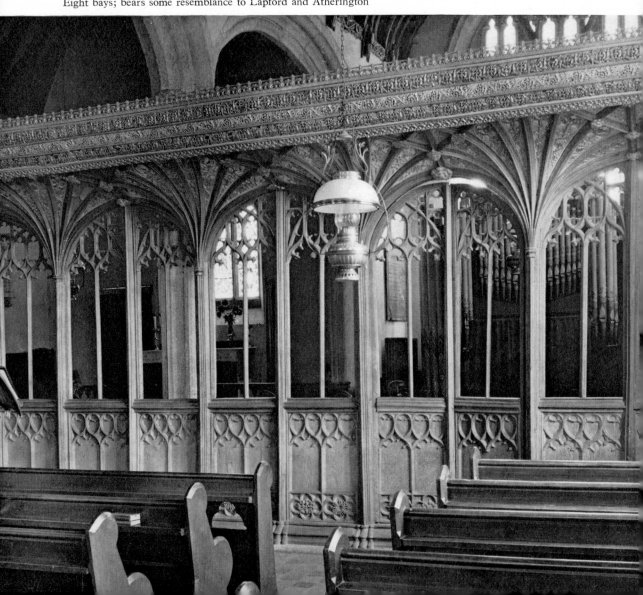

mouth); of St Catherine with her wheel (Holne and Widecombe-in-the-Moor). At Combe Martin and Manaton we can see St Margaret of Antioch emerging from the dragon's mouth; at Alphington, St Dunstan seizing the devil by the nose with a pair of tongs; at Alphington and Portlemouth, Sir John Schorne, holding a large boot in which he has imprisoned the devil. There is St Cecilia at Kenton, holding not an organ but a guitar; St Victor with his windmill (Torbryan); and at Kenn, St Bridget of Sweden writing her revelations at the dictation of the Holy Ghost.

The Wise Men, the Apostles, and the Prophets are to be seen at many places, and there is a fair sprinkling of little-known saints such at St Damien (Wolborough), St Erasmas (Cheriton Bishop), St Gudule (Bere Ferrers), St Eloy (Ashton), and St Ursula (Kenn and Manaton). At Wolborough, there is St Paul the Hermit; at Hennock, St Winifred;

and at Berry Pomeroy, St Thaddaeus. St Simon Zelotes can be seen at Chudleigh, St Sebastian at Kenton, St Zita at Plymtree, and, for good measure, there is St Louis (Gidleigh), St Petronilla (Wolborough) and St Placid (Chivelstone).

An unusual treatment of the wainscot is to be seen at certain places. At Bridford and Lustleigh, for instance, the panels are carved from top to bottom with small figures in relief. At Marwood and Warkleigh, there are medallions accompanied by Renaissance arabesque, while Littleham (near Exmouth), Sutcombe and Swimbridge, have wainscot panels entirely composed of late Gothic tracery or vertical strips of foliage. The latter closely resemble horizontal trails and have an affinity with a type of ornament characteristic of several Cornish screens.

Plymtree, retaining its ancient colour-decoration, is characteristic of the fan-vaulted Devon screen

Harberton: fifteenth-century stone pulpit
carved and painted to match the screen, the latter restored in 1871

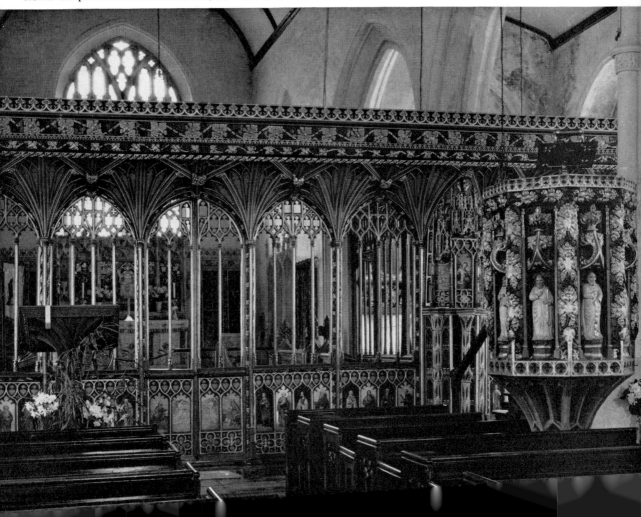

(Exe Valley type) and is acknowledged by many to be the finest. Exceptionally well preserved, though not so elaborate as Atherington, so delicate as Kentisbeare, nor so rich in detail as Lapford or South Pool, it is nevertheless magnificently carved and was, in all probability, erected shortly after 1470 by Isabel, widow of Humphrey Stafford, Earl of Devon. She subsequently married Sir Thomas Bourchier, second son of Lord John Berners, and the Bourchier knot appears on two bosses on the front. The screen does not appear to fit the church, having been shortened at the north, and is thought to have been removed from some abbey.

Uffculme's screen, 67 ft wide and extending across nave and aisles, is the longest in the county. It is similar to the one at Halberton, which has been dated as 1420. Nearby, at Kentisbeare, is a screen of singular beauty, a work of the highest order, both in the delicacy of its varied design and the vigour of its execution. Of the Exe Valley type, it appears to have been a model for many others from Halse and Combe St Nicholas in Somerset in the east, to Chumleigh—where the rise of vaulting is unusually high—in the west. Each of the ten bays

of Kentisbeare is different, whereas the majority of the Exe Valley type repeat the design of a single bay. Kenton's screen (enriched Perpendicular), is the prototype of numerous others in the county. Of massive and stately proportions, it shows surprising evidence of Flemish handiwork, although it was probably completed locally after erection. Surprising because, unlike Norfolk and Suffolk, there is little evidence of Flemish influence in the screens of Devon.

The roodscreen at Kenton is responsible for a projecting stair-turret giving access to the loft. This is also a prominent feature of some other churches, as at Malborough, Manaton and Woodbury and, by breaking the line of an aisle wall, provides external indication of the distinction, marked internally by the screen, between the aisle and its eastern chapel. The turret at Throwleigh is remarkably decorated, and embattled examples can be seen at Little Hempston, Stockland and Torbryan.

The high standard of local craftsmanship in woodcarving is well illustrated by the thirteen-bay roodscreen of Berry Pomeroy. Crossing nave and both aisles, it is 46 ft in length and, according to

Ashton: parclose screen painting. A remarkable and unique series of prophets, c 1525

Lysons, still retained its roodloft in 1822. Bridford's screen, erected in the early part of the reign of Henry VIII by its vicar, Walter Southcote, is notable both for its colour and for the lavish detail of its carving. For sheer size, none can compete with Hartland, c 1470, where the screen is 48 ft long, the width of the roodloft nearly 6 ft, and the full height 12 ft. Lapford's screen, of early sixteenth-century date, contains much beautiful detail and though similar to the one at Atherington, the cornices more nearly resemble those of Hartland. The Dartmouth type, as can be seen in the town's St Saviour, is justly celebrated and its early fifteenth-century tracery is typical of the southern district, having ogee canopies with carved crockets and finials over each pair of lights under the arcaded heads. The vaulting ribs are very substantial and enriched with a scroll pattern.

The screen at Swimbridge—one of the earliest, and well restored in 1887—is notable for the bold and massive character of its general design. It incorporates some very rich yet delicate carving, and the fan vaulting is singularly fine. In some respects, it resembles both Hartland and Lapford. Still in position overhead are the remains of the ancient rood-beam, now supporting a trumpeting angel. Here, too, can be seen a rood window—often deemed necessary to illuminate the great rood and usually constructed on the south side. Other examples are to be found at Barnstaple, St Peter; at Tawstock and at Ilfracombe, where a pair of modern dormers were erected in 1899.

The rood-beam, still *in situ*, can also be seen at Cullompton, far above the loft and quite out of reach, but here the great rood is believed to have been suspended, since it footed upon a carved

Payhembury: roodscreen detail. *c* 1450.
In good preservation; coving, cornice and cresting complete

'Golgotha' which rested on the floor of the rood-loft. The screen, to nave and aisles, is of the ordinary Perpendicular type, with the customary form of tracery.

No survey of Devon screenwork, however brief, could be complete without reference to the magnificent Beer-stone screen of Totnes erected by order of the Corporation between 1459 and 1460 in order to divide the chancel from the church by freestone, as at the cathedral in Exeter. A roodloft of unusual depth and capacity formerly stood over the screen, which was replaced in the eighteenth century by a Georgian gallery with pews which, in turn, was removed during the Restoration by Sir Gilbert Scott. This church had a peculiar arrangement for giving access to the roodloft. Instead of being in the aisle walls, the stairs were contrived within the chancel, being entered beneath a traceried bay or polygonal projection on the north side, just eastward of the choir seats. There was a gallery of approach to the loft, extending all along the top of the north parclose screen. This and the main gallery both had a flat panelled soffit, enriched with diagonal ribs and bosses. This is described and illustrated by Lysons, who refers to the screens as bearing tabernacle work, painted and gilded.

The development of the roodscreen, like the parish church itself, was an expression of the faith of the common people and these works of art were objects of pride to wealthy town merchant and village peasant alike. The congregations in many a Devon church in those days must have been fascinated, and inspired, by such remarkable examples of the skill and artistry of their fellow men, and we are indeed fortunate that so much has survived.

Colebrooke: parclose screen. Of definite French influence. The same carver worked at Brushford and Coldridge

9. Pulpits and Bench-Ends

Pulpits, or perhaps simply lecterns, were in use as early as the twelfth century at Canterbury, Bury St Edmunds and Beaulieu Abbey. In the Early English and Decorated periods stone pulpits were to be found in the refectories of Chester Cathedral and the old abbey of Shrewsbury, but it was not until the close of the fifteenth century that pulpits were erected in our parish churches. Still later they proliferated under the influence of the Reformation and the growing importance of the sermon in church services until, eventually, the edict of 1547

called for their provision in all churches where they were not already in being. Often, they took the place of the roodloft when the latter was used for music, but in two Devon parishes at least—Malborough and West Alvington—the pulpit is known to have stood upon the roodloft until as late as the nineteenth century.

Having been so successful in transforming grim and dark interiors with rich and delicately carved screens, it was natural that Devon's native wood-carvers and stonemasons should be called upon to

Dittisham: pulpit. Very fine medieval
stone example

exercise their skill upon the pulpit which, in many cases, stood cheek by jowl with the roodscreen. The result, in the main, was the evolution of a design quite distinctive in character and one in which tracery plays only a minor part. As a rule, they are encrusted with leaf decoration, the main panels incorporate small carved figures under nodding ogee canopies, or triangularly projecting canopies, and they have either thickly foliated buttresses, or even more thickly foliated frames between them. Several post-Reformation examples in the county are enriched by the spoils of the roodlofts, if not constructed from their remains, as at Alwington, Kingsbridge, Shebbear and Sherford. All are characteristic of Devon and only at Pilton is there one of a type common to all England.

Pride of place must go to the stone pulpits. Only sixty medieval stone pulpits are left in all England, and eleven of these are in Devon. The finest is at Dittisham, gleaming in gold and still retaining its original, blue-painted figures of John the Baptist and four companions in their canopied niches. Singularly small, it stands on a graceful stem, offering a fine example of the chalice form. The pulpit at Witheridge, according to Oliver, was originally in the cathedral at Exeter, but was removed when thought to be in danger from Puritan iconoclasts. Of the best Devon type, it has rich foliated scrolls bordering the panels, which contain statuary under fine canopy work.

Holne: pulpit.
Unusual design on a goblet foot.
Eight coats of arms are displayed

Pilton: stone pulpit.
Late Perpendicular. Elizabethan
oak canopy, hour glass on iron hand

Of medieval pulpits in wood, of which there are about one hundred in the country as a whole, Devon has no fewer than twenty. One of the rarest examples is preserved at Chivelstone, in the South Hams. Of early sixteenth-century origin, it is small —only 3 ft wide and little more than 4 ft high— and each panel is just over ten inches wide. It has been carved, except for the hinged door of two panels, out of a single block of oak and is without join or break. Octagonal in plan, it is richly painted with red, green, black and white, and some traces of gold. The shields, on a field of red, bear a sort of label in four rows; alternately a crowned 'M' in black and a carnation in gold, with the exception of one of the two on the pulpit door. Each of the panels shows a distinctive treatment of the foliage,

and the crocketting is reminiscent of what may be called the conventional Decorated ornament, with a freedom and vigour rarely found in Perpendicular work. Chivelstone, the only church in England dedicated to the fourth-century pope, St Sylvester, has much to interest the ecclesiologist.

In many respects, the Chivelstone pulpit is similar to the one at Holne, which incorporates the arms of the Abbey of Buckfast and those of Bishop Oldham, as well as commemorating the marriage of William Bourchier—probably its donor—with the heiress of Hankford. It was erected about 1510, at the same time as the screen. East Allington, probably coeval with the screen (1547), resembles in many respects the well-known stone pulpit of Dartmouth, St Saviour, and is quite probably a copy. Under the canopies of the flat niches on each face are various royal and aristocratic badges, while the enriched moulding at the foot carries a series of shields. It has a wealth of rich detail, including roses, thistles, faces peeping from foliage, lions, griffins, and other curious animals.

The pulpit at Kenton is noteworthy as a careful duplication of the original that was destroyed by Ashworth in the restoration of 1865. For many years some of its carving lay forgotten in a cupboard in the village schoolroom, until it was rescued and the pulpit reconstructed by Herbert Read. As a boy, the Reverend Sabine Baring Gould made a drawing to scale and it was this that made the complete restoration possible. The artistic merit of the old work is second to none in the country, and the carver has admirably captured the spirit of the ancient work in his reproduction of the missing portions.

At Swimbridge—a treasure-house of carving in both stone and wood—the hexagonal stone pulpit stands on a tall pedestal with carved saints and angels, and still bears traces of its original colouring. Its cup-shaped form and small dimensions are characteristic of the latter part of the fifteenth century. North Molton's pulpit of oak, c 1450, has been praised by many authorities. It has canopied niches, a carved cornice and vertical scrolls, but the figures of Peter and John, and of the Good Shepherd, are modern. It has a fine early Hanoverian sounding board with inlaid and richly carved cornice and soffit and, above it, a trumpeting angel.

The sixteenth-century stone pulpit of Pilton, previously mentioned, is interesting for its Elizabethan oak canopy, and for the hour-glass held out by a white-painted iron hand about two feet long. Tawstock has a similar hour-glass, which was used by the parson in most of our parish churches at this time to regulate the length of his sermon. Ashton, good Jacobean and complete with an elaborate sounding board, has an iron stand but the hour-glass itself is missing.

Pulpits of more recent times have not always received the attention they deserve, and there are several good examples in the county from the seventeenth and eighteenth centuries. One such is at Langtree, carved with garlands and cherubs' heads, and there is another at Exbourne, dated 1665 and the work of Simon Westlake, whose family lived at Woodhall, Exbourne, for over 500 years. Its entrance, direct from the vestry, is unique. Other examples of these years are the 'two-decker' with canopy at Morchard Bishop, the 'three-deckers' of Branscombe and Molland, and the wooden pulpit

of Ottery St Mary (1722), carved with figures of the Evangelists in the panels. The carver was William Culne, 'of this parish', who proudly claims in the inscription—'All this in every part was done by me'. It formerly had a canopy surmounted by a gilded trumpeting angel, which now adorns the top of the medieval clock.

Crediton's pulpit of Mansfield stone, bearing the figures of the four Evangelists, was erected in 1887, while from the beginning of the present century we have had the beautiful 'missionary' pulpit of Dunchideock, the work of Herbert Read of Exeter. Here are the carved figures of Our Lord, Saints Columba (the missionary of Scotland), Augustine (the missionary of England), Boniface (the missionary of Germany who was born at Crediton in the year 680), and Petrock, the Cornish saint. Its rich and elaborate carving depicts birds pecking at grapes, snails, a caterpillar, and a beetle. At Lewtrenchard, the pulpit, also modern (1900) but based upon medieval design, bears a strong resemblance to Kenton.

Seating in churches did not become fashionable until the Perpendicular period. Previously, it had been the custom to stand when not kneeling, though there were stone benches against the walls in some churches for the use of the aged or infirm. Sexes were strictly separated; men on the south side, women on the north. The West of England is the proud possessor of a great many bench-ends, and Devon, celebrated for its number and variety, is no less rich in this type of woodcarving than its neighbours, Cornwall and Somerset. Bench-end carvings often indicate the ownership of pews, many being carved with initials, whilst others show a surname or heraldic coat of arms. Occasionally, the pew owner is identified by means of a carving representing his trade or occupation.

The West Country type of pew is a rectangular block of oak (or chestnut, as at Braunton) whose squared top rises little, if at all, above the back of the seat and whose outer surface is richly ornamented with elaborate and varied patterns and subjects. The range is very wide—animals, emblems of the Passion, flowers, hagiology, mermaids, patterned foliage, ships, tracery and vines. Sometimes they incorporate humorous details, such as faces in the centres of flowers and little animals amongst the foliage. Most date from the latter part of the fifteenth century to late in the sixteenth century, though there is some fine modern work, such as the nineteenth-century choir stalls designed by Sedding at Holbeton—a veritable feast of fruit and flowers, birds and animals. Bench backs and fronts are also occasionally preserved, as at Ashton and Braunton.

The most remarkable and varied series of bench-ends is probably that of Lapford. Dated *c* 1540, they incorporate distinctive Renaissance work, similar to that which can be seen on the roodscreen. Particularly noticeable is the characteristic union of these Renaissance details with purely Gothic forms and workmanship. An interesting feature are three pairs of heads in profile, male and female facing each other. This was a favourite and distinctive feature of the work of this particular period and was possibly intended as portraits of the respective owners. A similar series of the same date can be seen at Down St Mary.

Pevsner has illustrated, by a comparison of known dates, the advent of the Italian influence. Hartland of 1530 and Northlew of 1537 have no Renaissance motifs, whereas Dowland of 1546 has. The type is unchanged at Braunton—dates between 1560 and 1593 are recorded—as it is at Alwington, where the date 1580 appears. Much of this later woodcarving was by the same workmen or from the same workshops. Free guilds were becoming more active and influential as producers of work, and it is a fair assumption that secular schools were largely employed in the execution of this class of work.

Holbeton: bench end. Evidence that the skill of some modern carvers is equal to that of their medieval predecessors

Of the many medieval examples of bench-ends, those of Abbotsham, Combe-in-Teignhead, East Budleigh, High Bickington and Lewtrenchard take high place. Those at Abbotsham, of the early sixteenth century, are again varied—emblems of the Passion, the Crucifixion (a rare subject), a juggler, two full-length saints, the Bourchier knot and ornamental initials. One has a builder's compass and square, another depicts a man sitting backwards on a horse, bow in hand. Drunkenness is symbolised by a chained ape; death by a gruesome figure. The mitred bishop with a model of the church in his hand is thought to be John Veysey, Bishop of Exeter.

Bench-ends in the north transept of Combe-in-Teignhead are exceptionally noteworthy. Here, richly-carved panels are surmounted by diminutive quadrupeds; while the three sides are surrounded by broad strips of foliage or flowers, the bottom corners terminating in human faces. At the base are elaborate quatrefoils, and each of the niched figures is surmounted by a quatrefoiled head. One example incorporates four saints (St George, St Agnes, St Hubert and St Genest) carved in four separate panels. Two of the ends have single central figures—St Catherine, with her wheel and sword; St Mary Magdalene, with her long flowing hair and her jar of spikenard.

At East Budleigh, sixty-three bench-ends remain *in situ;* the date 1537 inscribed on one of them shows when the church was seated. Their fame is due not so much to the design and quality of work, but rather for their extent and intimate association with the Raleigh family. In no two cases is the

Lapford: bench end. Man holding a knotted whip. One of a series illustrating the Sacred Passion of Christ

Abbotsham: bench end. The Crucifixion.
The faces of Mary (left) and John
have been deliberately defaced

carving alike; all are vigorously and boldly carved with motifs of leaves, shears, angels, faces in profile, a three-masted ship, and the armorial bearing of the Raleighs and their neighbours, the St Cleres of Tidwell, Arcot, Chiverston, Courtenay, Ford and Grenville. High Bickington boasts about seventy bench-ends, c 1520-40; some in late Gothic style, others with Renaissance detail; many are carved with figures of saints. Stabb tells us that when the west gallery was removed those now occupying the west end of the nave were retrieved from farmhouses in the neighbourhood where they had been used for a variety of purposes. Particularly fascinating is the modern carving on the choir stalls,

with its procession of animals and birds.

At Lewtrenchard, one bench-end in the north aisle has a vigorous St Michael trampling on a dragon and weighing souls in scales, while quaint heads peep out of the top of the scales. Other examples represent the embattled gateway of a castle, with a curious bearded man's head about it; a full-length saint with right hand raised in blessing and carrying a ball in his left hand; and a whimsical figure, possibly intended for St Genest, the jester saint. There is also the figure of Christ, shields bearing the instruments of Christ's Passion, tracery, and coats of arms. Another magnificent series of eighty-four can be seen at Braunton, one of which depicts the church's patron saint, St Brannoc.

Fine examples of manorial pews are to be seen at Poltimore and Tawstock. Arthur Mee has recalled the scene at Poltimore a century ago when the last of the Bampfyldes, the second Baron Poltimore, 'marched to church on Sundays with his servants, the men in top hats, the women in poke bonnets'. Immediately after the Reformation, the Bampfyldes appropriated for themselves the roodloft, and retained possession of it until the eighteenth century when they built their own special pew, 7 ft from the floor and partly over the south transept, to which they gained access by way of the original roodloft stairway. Panelled in oak, it had a moulded ceiling, red cloth lining, comfortably cushioned seats, and a small fireplace. When the south aisle was built and the screen removed in 1874, a new staircase had to be constructed to give access to the pew, which is now the vestry. The north transept was formerly provided with a somewhat similar gallery pew, for use of retainers of the Bampfylde family.

The family pew in the south transept of Tawstock is small with two solid backwalls panelled, and a complete ceiling with rosettes. The decoration, especially the thick baluster, is decidedly in the Franco-Flemish Early Renaissance taste. Manorial pews, like much else remaining in our ancient churches, are enduring evidence of the one-time wealth and influence of the local squirearchy.

East Budleigh: bench end. Probably a wool-merchant's pew, depicting an angel, a woolstapler's shears and a teasel holder

10. Monuments & Brasses

Few churches are without monuments of one sort or another, and, most frequently, they are memorials to the squirearchy, lawyers, wealthy merchants, and local priests, or to citizens who returned from overseas wars. Unfortunately, our medieval forebears swept away a great many earlier monuments during the great rebuilding to make way for resting-places for their own generation. Thus there are no surviving tombs of Norman date,

and only very few of the Early English period. Many were destroyed or defaced under the Puritan regime, especially sepulchral brasses, which were stripped wholesale from the pavements. Still more were destroyed during the 'restorations' of the nineteenth century.

As Cornelius writes in his Devonshire Association paper (1951), the practice of burial within churches 'at first reserved for the very few, increased

Haccombe: toy tomb. The son of the lord of the manor. Late fourteenth century

through the Middle Ages until, after the Reformation it reached its peak in the seventeenth and eighteenth centuries'. By then, it had become an abuse by means of which churchwardens levied 'pit money' and our parish churches became honeycombed with graves and stocked with putrefying human remains which were frequently disturbed for fresh arrivals, to the detriment of the health of the living.

At first, sepulchre in parish churches was apparently confined to the lord of the manor (frequently the founder and patron) and his family, and perhaps to the parish priest. Ultimately, it became the practice for anyone who could afford it to be buried within the church. The position of honour was on the north side of the sanctuary, and here was frequently buried the church's founder,

or the one mainly responsible for its rebuilding. His tomb also served, at times, as an Easter Sepulchre, and it is in the Perpendicular chancel chapels that most of these tombs and memorials are now to be found.

For centuries, English craftsmen in wood, stone, metal, alabaster and marble specialized in monuments. 'English sculpture,' wrote J. B. Rouquet in 1755, after thirty years' sojourn among aritsts in England, 'has hitherto been almost wholly monumental.' The earlier examples in Devon's parish churches are the thirteenth-century effigies to be seen at Atherington, Georgeham and Iddesleigh, three remote parishes which only comparatively recently have awakened from their medieval slumber. All three sets of effigies are crosslegged, which was once thought to indicate that the de-

Feniton: cadaver. Possibly one of the Malherbe family, c 1450

Colyton: Beaufort monument.
Margaret Beaufort, Countess of
Devon, 1449. One of several fine
monuments to be seen here

ceased had been on a crusade, though how such a
fallacy came about is unknown. The device is
common only in England and was probably adopted
simply to show the lines of the figure to best
advantage.

The knight in armour at Atherington (north
chancel aisle) is Sir William Champernowne of
Umberleigh and the one at Georgeham (south
chancel chapel) Mauger St Aubyn, who died in
1294. This church, incidentally, has an unusually
fine, though badly damaged, panel of the
Crucifixion, c 1300. The Iddesleigh effigy (north
chancel chapel) is unfortunately hidden by the

organ. Of a date around 1250, it is probably of a
Sully—who, at this period were squires of Iddes-
leigh—and no doubt an ancestor of the redoubtable
Sir John Sully who is buried at Crediton.

The best monuments of the Decorated period
are those of Broadclyst, Haccombe and Ottery St
Mary. The stone knight of Broadclyst—seen
beneath a canopied sedilia—is one of the finest of
its kind and commemorates Sir Roger de Nonant,
the last of the Norman lords of this parish, who
died around 1340. Fascinating, too, is the collection
to be seen at Haccombe—a mausoleum of the lords
of the manor, furnishing examples of the armour

and costume of the Middle Ages ranging from a thirteenth-century mailed knight (Sir Stephen Haccombe) to a seventeenth-century brass of Thomas and Ann Carew. A diminutive alabaster effigy, for long supposed to be that of Edward Courtenay, son of Sir Hugh and Phillipa Courtenay is, judging by the apparel, at least fifty years earlier and of the late fourteenth century. Little more than two feet in length—'a toy figure on a toy tomb', as Arthur Mee has described it—there is nothing like it in the rest of the county. Three other monuments at Haccombe are also of fourteenth-century date.

At Ottery St Mary, the two ogee-headed canopied tombs—with cusping and richly-carved foliage—of Otho de Grandisson (died 1358) and his wife Beatrice (died 1374) stand opposite each other and are among the best of their period in the West of England. The head of Beatrice is supported by the outspread wings of two angels, whilst at her feet are two dogs, emblems of fidelity. The ogee-canopy of each monument has fifty shields for arms.

Apart from the Kirkham chantry sculpture at Paignton, Devon produced little of outstanding merit or interest in the fifteenth century. There was plenty of variety but little of good quality, and what there is is more impressive for its decorative rather than its sculptural qualities. Of some interest are the cadavers to be seen at Feniton and Paignton, corpse-like figures depicted in the last stage of emaciation and partly covered with a shroud—no doubt to remind worshippers that this life does not last for ever. The figure at Feniton is well carved and well preserved, and could depict a member of the Malherbe family. The one at Paignton is popularly supposed to represent a bishop of Raphoe in Ireland, who acted as suffragan bishop of the diocese and is known to have died in Paignton in about 1450. The tomb-chest of Sir William Hankford (1422) at Monkleigh—there is no effigy on the lid—affords some indication of the quality of the work which could be wrought. It is decorated with seven pinnacles, ogee-arched niches; the recess in which it is placed is exceptionally finely cusped and displays well-carved cresting. Perhaps the most ambitious medieval monument in north Devon is the canopied tomb at Ashwater of Thomas Carminow (died 1443) and his wife. When their two daughters succeeded to the manor, they lengthened the south aisle by adding a chapel at the east.

As those who had financed the great sixteenth-century rebuilding died, so they were given a place of honour, and many of their monuments remain. Among them may be counted those memorials to

the Bassets of Umberleigh (at Atherington); Sir Richard Pomeroy of Berry Pomeroy; the Carews of Bickleigh (near Tiverton); and Sir Lewis Pollard at Bishops Nympton. The monument to Thomas Andrew at Exeter, St Mary Arches—he was mayor in 1505 and 1510—is the only pre-seventeenth-century example in the city outside the cathedral, indicative of the wholesale destruction which took place at Exeter in 1646. Among others in the county are the memorials to Henry Beaumont at Gittisham; Richard Coffin, Sheriff of Devon in 1493, at Heanton Punchardon; the Chichesters of Pilton; and the Bampfyldes of Poltimore.

In monumental sculpture, Gothic detail died hard in Devon. The tomb-chest of John Waldron (1579) at Tiverton, St Peter, is still entirely Gothic, without trace of Renaissance feeling. The same can be said of the tombs of those sixteenth-century rectors of South Pool and Woodleigh, Thomas Briant and Thomas Smythe, which now occupy the Easter Sepulchres in the two churches. At Chagford, the tomb of Sir John Wyddon (1575) is still Early Renaissance, except for some odd cusping which consists of strapwork elements. The Perpendicular era still lingers on in its foliage decoration.

The multiplicity of monuments after the Reformation, particularly during the seventeenth century, becomes astonishing, no less in Devon than in other counties. 'This Protestant sculpture', as Sacheverell Sitwell has called it, came of an age when the building of new churches had virtually ceased. At last, the great tide of architectural activity had ebbed; its tombs and monuments are among its few ecclesiastical reminders.

Apart from the collection of Tawstock, and a few individual pieces (notably at Cadeleigh, Colyton, Eggesford, Marystow, Newton St Cyres and Wembury) there is little in Devon to compare with the Home Counties or the work of the Bristol, Gloucester and Hereford schools. The finest work in the country was commissioned from London, but because of Devon's conservatism and desire to keep faith with the local craftsmen working in Beer stone and alabaster—sometimes called the Exeter school—little came into the county from outside. One of the very few examples is the memorial to Sir Thomas Putt (died 1686) at Gittisham, attributed by Mrs Esdaile to William Kidwell. It is a big tomb-chest with white marble vases, under an arched recess of black marble, and Pevsner sums it up as 'cold, competent, expensive and metropolitan'. There is virtually nothing in the county attributable to the great craftsmen of the period, such as Maximilian Colt and Nicholas Stone. Stone was born at Woodbury in 1586 and lived for some time at Sidbury. He became a pupil of Inigo Jones and went on to become master-mason to King James and King Charles.

The Leach monument at Cadeleigh (1637) is the largest of its type in Devon. Restored by public subscription in 1903, it shows Sir Simon Leach and his wife, full length recumbent figures beneath a high canopy, together with the kneeling figures of their nine children. Colyton is noted for its monuments, and among the best are those of Margaret Beaufort, Countess of Devon (1449), which is typical of the period; and to Sir John Pole (1658)

and his wife (1628). The Pole monument—free standing with an eight-column canopy—is still entirely in the Elizabethan tradition, but there is a suggestion here, unsupported by any documentary evidence, of Gerard Johnson or William Cure of the Southwark school. There are other Pole monuments in the south chancel chapel.

At Eggesford, the memorials to Lord Edward Chichester (died 1648), his wife (died 1616), and their son Arthur, Earl of Donegal (died 1650), are all good examples of carving in alabaster. The Donegal carving has been attributed to William Wright. Perhaps the most ambitious monument in

Newton St Cyres: Northcote monument. The chief attraction of this neatly thatched village. John Northcote of Hayne, 1632

the county is the Renaissance free standing monument to Sir Thomas Wise (1630) at Marystow, and the Northcote monument (1632) at Newton St Cyres the most striking. John Northcote is shown in full armour; busts of his two wives appear in medallions on either side, while beneath are the kneeling figures of their children. For sheer bulk, there is little to compare with the large monument in limestone to Sir John Hele (1608) at Wembury, which rises from floor to ceiling and takes up the north side of the chancel.

The monument collection at Tawstock, particularly notable for its seventeenth-century work, is too important to dismiss without a detailed list and deserves wider national attention than it has yet received. A preservation as extensive as this is all too rare and has been due in great part to the

manor's descent by inheritance through some thirty-one successive generations, unbroken by any alienation or forfeiture—a truly remarkable record. Also preserved at Tawstock are some fine seventeenth-century examples of decorative hatchments by heraldic painters.

THE TAWSTOCK COLLECTION

Fourteenth century.
North chancel chapel. Effigy of a lady, possibly Eleanor or Margaret Martice.

1589   South chancel chapel. Frances, Lady Fitzwarren. Six-poster with recumbent effigy (one of the largest in the county)

1597   North transept. Sir John Wray. Slate-covered tomb-chest

Tawstock : mainly fourteenth century.
It houses one of the most remarkable monument collections

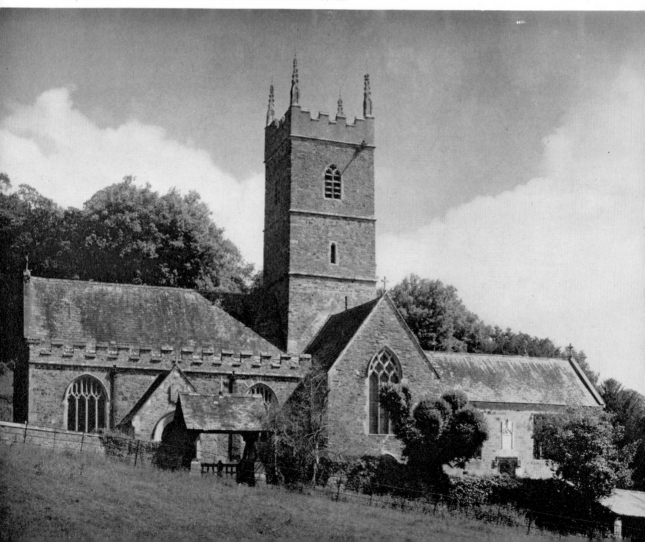

Tawstock: Fitzwarren monument.
Frances Lady Fitzwarren, 1589. Impressive for its size

1614   South chancel chapel. Thomas Hinson and wife. Kneeling figures facing each other

1623   Chancel. William Bourchier, third Earl of Bath. Standing wall monument of alabaster. Good work of its date. Has been attributed to Maximilian Colt but there is no documentary proof of this

1631   Chancel. Mary St John. Epitaph with kneeling figure

1633   Chancel. William Skippon. Epitaph with kneeling figure

1680   South chancel chapel. Henry Bourchier, fifth Earl of Bath. In the new Italian manner which, incidentally, had little influence on Devon sculpture. Remarkable free standing monument of black and white marble

1680   South chancel chapel. Lady Rachel Fane, wife of the fifth Earl. Life-size standing figure in white marble (attributed by Mrs Esdaile to Balthasar Burman)

1729   North transept. Henry Northcote, by Thomas Jewill of Barnstaple

1751   South transept. Mary Lady Wray. White and pink marble sarcophagus on rocaille feet

1758   North transept. Ann Chilcot. Inscription surmounted by a tondo with a seated allegorical figure. Fine piece of its date

1784   South transept. Sir Bourchier Wray. Free standing urn on a big square pedestal

Also in the collection are many lesser epitaphs by Gould and Young of Barnstaple, Stephens of Exeter and King of Bath.

In addition to its larger and more ambitious works, the Exeter school also produced some interesting small monuments. Representative examples of these include the Blake monument at Barnstaple, St Peter; and the little alabaster at Newton St Cyres representing Sherland Shore (1632). Other examples, often with frontal demi-figures in niches or oval medallions, can be found at Alwington, Combe Martin, East Down, Kenton, and Swimbridge. Big epitaphs with columns, pediments and leaf scrolls, or garlands in the Wren-Gibbons style are frequent, e g Clovelly, and some good work by an interesting early eighteenth-century Devon sculptor, Weston, can be seen at Exeter, St Martin; Ashprington and Whitchurch.

Pevsner is, of course, right in dismissing Devon as a county of brasses, but enough remain to furnish us with examples of nearly every kind. They range from the simple plate, unadorned except for any artistic quality that the lettering may display, to the complete effigy, or effigies, under architectural canopies, the whole surrounded by an inscribed border fillet. Brasses are far more numerous in England than in any other country. The Reverend W. F. Creeny (1884) estimated that there were more than 4,000 engraved brasses left in England from some 150,000 originally laid down. The earliest are easily the finest, in boldness of design, in accuracy of workmanship, and in excellence of material.

Excluding those in the cathedral at Exeter, just under 100 dated monumental brasses remain in Devon. At Stoke Fleming, the brass to John Corp (1351) and his granddaughter Eleanor Corp (1391) is the earliest dated in the West of England. They stand beneath a rich canopy ornamented with quatrefoils, battlemented, and with lanthorn lights at the ends and in the centre. Dressed in the civilian style of the period, both have their hands joined in prayer. The brass memorial plate to Elias Newcomen, a seventeenth-century rector of Stoke Fleming (and great-grandfather of Thomas Newcomen of Dartmouth, inventor of the steam engine), declares that he was 'in knowledge old, in zeal of life most grave'. In nearby Dartmouth, St Saviour, there is a particularly interesting brass memorial to a wealthy merchant, John Hawley (1408), and his two wives. Seven times mayor of Dartmouth, Hawley was largely responsible for building the chancel.

The only fourteenth-century brass in the county, apart from Stoke Fleming, is in the chancel of Stoke-in-Teignhead, c 1375. It depicts a priest arrayed in mass vestments comprising alb, chasuble, manaple and stole. Although not visible, the back was engraved in 1496 with the figure of another priest, so that it is, in fact, a palimpsest, a term derived from the Greek words meaning 'again scraped'. Another example of a palimpsest can be seen at Yealmpton. One side is engraved to Isobel Copleston 1580, while on the other side there is a fragmentary Flemish engraving of the fifteenth-century priest in whose memory the brass was originally made. Another part of this figure has been identified under the altar at Denham, near Eye, Suffolk, but how and why part was brought to Yealmpton is unknown.

Devon's Perpendicular period brasses are best exemplified by the 33-inch high figure of Sir Nicholas Carew (1469) at Haccombe. The armour includes a 'vizored salard' (a steel skull-cap), a sword and dagger, and the feet are shod in sollerets, to which are attached rowelled spurs. At the angles of the brass are shields bearing the Carew arms.

Four other brasses at Haccombe span, collectively, a period of nearly 200 years.

The majority of Devon brasses are of the late sixteenth and seventeenth centuries. Generally speaking, they are not of a high order, the best being those to John Roope (1609), Dartmouth, St Petrock, and to Mary Dowrish (1604) at Sandford. Mary Dowrish, sister to George Carew, first and only Earl of Totnes, is depicted on an altar tomb with her four kneeling children, and surrounded by twenty-one shields. At East Allington, there are two interesting Tudor brasses; one of a kneeling woman with pointed headdress and fur-trimmed gown; the other to John Fortescue (died 1595) and his wife Honor, who is wearing an embroidered gown with a flowing skirt.

Tawstock : Fane monument. Lady Rachel Fane, wife of the fifth Earl of Bath, 1680

II. Post-Reformation

I. CLASSICAL AND EARLY REVIVAL GOTHIC

After the Reformation, and again after Mary's efforts to restore Catholic ritual and furnishings (1553-8), English churches suffered irreparable harm at the hands of the reformers. In Devon, the damage was mainly due to the desecration which took place during and after the Civil War (mid-seventeenth century) together with the work carried out in the name of 'restoration' and the vandalism let loose in the name of 'improvement'.

Despite all this, however, the Classical period (1620-1820), famed for its English country houses, also produced several interestingly new Devon churches and not all 'improvements'—largely the result of rising population and increasing wealth—were debased. Much of the seventeenth-century rebuilding only became necessary as a result of the neglect which had followed the 1550s—a period when many West Country churches were allowed to fall into disrepair. True, there were exceptions, for St Budeaux was built in 1563, the north aisle of Northam in 1593, and substantial rebuilding (nave piers, clerestory and chancel) took place at Tiverton, St Peter, between 1604 and 1606.

The city of Exeter, however, suffered particularly badly at the time, and many of its little sandstone churches seriously deteriorated. In the reign of King John there had been as many as twenty-eight, but in 1646 an ordnance of Parliament resulted in all but four (St Petrock, St Mary Major, St Mary Arches and St Edmund) being sold, or used as burying places or as schools. Happily, many were bought by their parishioners and, two years later, were returned to their proper parochial uses. But immense damage had been done and some never fully recovered. All Hallows on the Walls (included in Bishop Stapledon's Register for 1325) remained in a ruinous condition until the nineteenth century, when it was wholly removed and not replaced until 1845, when a new church of the same name was built on a site to the north of the old one.

It was not until the 1640s that the revival really started, a period which saw the building of Charles Church, Plymouth, the only completely new seventeenth-century church edifice; the rebuilding of Dartmouth, St Petrock; Exeter, St Thomas; Great Torrington; Woolsery (near Hartland); and the erection of the tower of Clyst Hydon. Only at Dartmouth, St Saviour, did 'improvement' come earlier, brought about by the unique and exceptionally close relationship of Church and Corporation, to whom it was sold in 1586 by Robert Peter, lord of the manor. This was a period of great prosperity for Dartmouth, booming from its lucrative trade with Newfoundland and Portugal, and lacking an adequate Guildhall, successive mayors lavished part of this prosperity on embellishments to their church. The record of their contributions is an impressive one: chancel 1616, tower (and remarkable south door of church with ironwork much older) 1631, west gallery 1633, north aisle rebuilt 1634, south aisle in 1635.

Charles Church, Plymouth, named in honour of King Charles I, was completed in 1658. Ruined by enemy action on the night of 20 March 1941, it was partially restored in 1952 and now stands as a memorial to Plymouth's 1,200 civilian dead of the second world war. It is post-Reformation Gothic, the chancel east window being a fine example of geometric tracery. Llewellyn Jewitt, writing in 1873, describes its interior as a mixture of both Gothic and Classical. 'The side aisles are each divided from the nave by a series of three arches, rising from clustered columns, and there are galleries on the north and south aisles and at the west end; the tall pulpit, with spiral staircase, stands in the centre. The altar screen, or reredos, is an arcade of nine arches, supported on marble pillars with foliated capitals.' The first spire, made of wood and covered with lead, was erected in 1708, but was superseded in 1767 by the stone spire.

Exeter, St Thomas, the largest of the city's parish churches—Gothic with sandstone west tower—was built in 1646, replacing a church dating back to 1412 which had been destroyed by fire the previous year. Present remains of the older building include the arcade with octagonal piers, plain octagonal capitals and double-chamfered arches. The north aisle was built in 1810 and the chancel nineteen years later. The rebuilding of Great Torrington in 1651 was made necessary by its virtual destruction on 16 February 1645 during the Civil War, when it was used by Royalists to store eighty barrels of gunpowder. The vestry (c 1485) survived in its entirety, and much of the fifteenth-century work in the old fabric was incorporated in the reconstruction, including a fine wagon-roof and pulpit. The present tower and spire date from 1830, when the old tower with its dome-shaped top were taken down. The eight bells are the finest of any in Devon's churches. Six were cast by Abel Rudhall of Gloucester in 1716, two were added later and all were re-hung in 1934.

For nearly a hundred years from the mid-seventeenth century, domestic and foreign politics, rather than ecclesiastical expression, excited the popular mind, though due credit should be given for such care as was taken and such building as was carried out. Repeated entries in churchwardens' accounts

Tiverton, St George: a notable Georgian church, 1730. The seating, pulpit and font are Victorian

Pinhoe: poor box. The parish beadle
in the time of Queen Anne, dated 1700

for work done upon roof and floor, walls and
windows (particularly where the medieval masons
had used Beer stone for external work) bear
witness to a watchfulness in this respect for which
succeeding generations must ever have been grateful. Roof repairs were a particularly constant source
of trouble and expense; thatch and shindells (slabs
of ragstone) were often replaced by roofing slates,
as at East Budleigh, Littleham (near Exmouth) and
Woodbury. 'Sodder' for 'worke about the ledds' is
a frequent item in the account books, and at East
Budleigh in 1673 the bill of the 'plumer' was £16
3s. Again, in 1705, the greater part of the lead had
to be renewed, together with the timber on which
it rested, the several bills amounting to £69 9s 11d.

The rebuilding of Cruwys Morchard in 1702,
after it had been 'consumed by lightning' on 13
February 1689, included installation of the classic-
style screen with Corinthian columns and a central
pediment. This is the latest screen in the diocese
until the Gothic revival of the nineteenth century,
and it is remarkable that a chancel screen should
have been regarded as a necessity in a remote
parish at such an early date as 1702.

Four new churches followed: Tiverton, St
George; St Aubyn's, Devonport; Teigngrace and
Filleigh. Tiverton and Teigngrace are of different
styles, though both are illustrative of the influence
of Wren. Neither has a true chancel but, instead,
a shallow sanctuary. Tiverton's church, the interior
now repainted in its original colours, was completed
in 1730. The plan is a plain rectangle of the Doric
order with galleries standing upon pillars and the
roof supported by two rows of Ionic columns. St
Aubyn's, Devonport (1771-2) is rectangular, with
tower and octagonal spire, and Teigngrace, built
by its patron, James Templer, in 1786, stands on
the site of the former church. Externally, the
building is Gothic, with a two-stage embattled west
tower of limestone (but with brick corbel table)
and a porch beneath. The interior, by contrast, is
very nearly Classical. Cruciform, with arms all of
equal length, the walls converge towards a central
dome-like roof. A west gallery supports the organ,
and until 1902 the tower had a slender spire.
Filleigh, erected in 1732 at the expense of Lord
Clinton and remodelled in 1876-7, has a dull
interior. The two-stage unbuttressed tower of the
old church remains.

The early years of the nineteenth century produced Princetown, built by French prisoners of
war in the Perpendicular style at the expense of
the Prince of Wales. (Was the architect Daniel
Alexander, who drew up the original plan of the

North Molton: chancel woodwork.
Exceptionally ornate 'Jacobean' chancel panelling, probably 1650

prison?); Exeter, St Sidwell, rebuilt 1812, destroyed during the second world war and now rebuilt on the same site; Exeter, Holy Trinity and Exeter, St David. Exeter, St David, designed by James Green and consecrated in 1816, had an oblong nave, west portico and cupola, and was notable as a fine example of the Greek revival. It was demolished in 1897 and an engraving of it can be seen in J. Britton's *Devonshire Illustrated*.

In South Street, Exeter, Holy Trinity, with its stucco front and tiny bell turret, was erected by Kendall in 1820. It replaced a demolished church on an ancient site where a church had stood since the twelfth century. The South Gate of the city, which adjoined it, was demolished at the same time. St Andrew's Chapel, Plymouth (1823), now St Catherine's Church and one of the few remaining public buildings designed by that great Plymouth architect, John Foulston, is severely Greek, a short-lived style altogether out of keeping with the Devon scene. It has a front of Dartmoor granite, without pediment, and still lacks the clock tower that was once projected.

Another Devon architect, Andrew Patey, was responsible for East Teignmouth and West Teignmouth, both causing a stir in the architectural world when they were erected in the early 1820s. Baring Gould called St James, West Teignmouth, 'hideous'; and Cresswell described it as 'an architectural monstrosity'. It is, nonetheless, an ingenious piece of engineering—an octagon with large windows (added to the fourteenth-century

Landcross : aisleless chapel of Norman origin.
Slate-hung bell turret, 1810

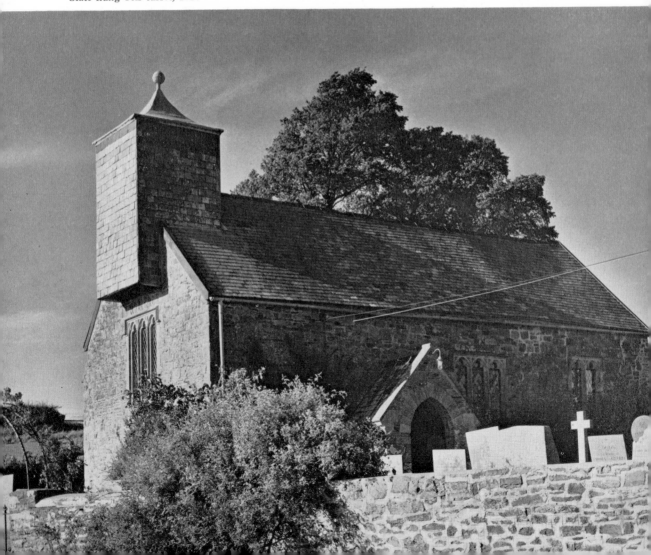

tower of the previous building), and a central lantern above a circular roof supported on tall, cast-iron pillars. Now restored and repainted, after being damaged during the second world war, it is a good example of its date, and must have seemed to its builders like a breath of fresh air after so much neglect of Devon's medieval heritage. The notable stone altar piece, also fourteenth-century work from the old church, contains twenty-nine small figures of saints in the carving.

The destruction of St Michael, East Teignmouth, was followed by the introduction of a neo-Norman nave—tall polygonal piers with block capitals but wagon roofs and fancy Perpendicular tracery. 'An almost unbelievable effort', was Pevsner's comment on it. The tower of three stages, designed by R.

Medley Fulford, was added in 1887. Constructed of limestone, with a plinth of dark red Kingsteignton stone and dressings of Doulton stone, it has buttresses set square and lofty, crocketed pinnacles.

This was the period when fittings began to bring 'a new look' to our churches. The term embraced altar rails, candelabra, floor tiles, galleries; oak panelling such as the Jacobean work in the chancel at North Molton; plaster ceilings of Italian character (Peamore chapel, Exminster, 1633); royal arms and 'three-decker' pulpits, clocks and sundials. It was also a period of organ-making, and two notable Devon families engaged in building them were the Chappyngtons of South Molton and the Loosemores of Bishops Nympton.

Altar rails were introduced gradually and became

Plymouth, St Catherine: by John Foulston 1823. The classical form lingered long in Devon

West Teignmouth: by Andrew Patey, 1820.
Thought to have been inspired by the octagon of Ely Cathedral

popular in the time of Archbishop Laud. Worthy of note are those with twisted balusters, such as Sampford Courtenay and West Putford, while Woodbury's are Elizabethan (c 1600) and marked by the entire absence of any survival of Gothic feeling. Although 'classical', an English sturdiness of character is retained, and this is especially noticeable in the proportions of the posts and buttresses that flank the central gates. Decorative floor tiles, made at Barnstaple, were used in many chancels and chapels, the usual motifs being a fleur-de-lys, lions, pelicans, roses and swans.

The galleries were integral parts of Stuart and Georgian churches. Where they were installed in Perpendicular interiors to accommodate the increasing population they were often unsightly—an obviously unplanned addition. The late survival of a magnificent tradition of woodcarving may be seen in the western gallery of Sandford (1657). It is comparable with the heavier gallery of Kentisbeare (1632) and the plain design of Dartmouth, St Saviour, with its painted shields of arms.

The arms of Charles II are particularly common in the West Country, though the earliest royal arms in Devon are those of Elizabeth I at Cheriton Bishop. Frithelstock has another excellent example in plaster, the work of John Abbot, a native of the parish, who was paid £13 6s 8d in 1677 for his labour. The county can also boast some remarkable sundials; the earliest is an Elizabethan one at Bampton, but the best are by John Berry of Muddiford, his masterpiece being that on the south porch of Tawstock. Dated 1757, it not only shows the signs of the Zodiac but also lines to indicate noon in different parts of the world, from Samarcand, Babylon, Jerusalem and Rome to Barbados. A similar dial, dated 1762, can be seen at Marwood. Of the 168 old churches in north Devon, sixty-eight still retain their sundials.

Other work of this period in the county and worthy of note includes :

1691 Meshaw. Tower (rest rebuilt 1838)
1695 St Giles in the Wood. Rebuilt (restored 1863)
1696 Pilton. Tower restored
1696 Tiverton, St Peter. Organ by Father Schmidt. Finest outside the Cathedral
1703 Bratton Fleming. Nave and north aisle rebuilt
1710 Stoke Damerel. Aisle added. Second aisle 1780, using 15 ft ship's stanchions as roof supports
1710 Kelly. South chancel aisle windows
1712 West Down. Tower rebuilt
1719 Sidbury. Restored
1724 Combe Martin. South porch built
1731 Welcombe. Tower built
1733 Merther. Enlargement of south aisle
1738 Brendon. Rebuilt
1740 c Morchard Bishop. Chancel rebuilt (round-headed windows). Reredos with Corinthian pilasters
1740 c Ashburton. Brass candelabra (particularly fine)
1741 Lynton. Nave reconstructed (north aisle 1817)
1743 Cheldon. Unique ornamental iron screen, formerly a mace rack
1752 Kings Nympton. Painted ceiling. Reredos with Ionic pilasters
1755 Beer. New aisle (church completely rebuilt 1877)
1765 Luffincott. Rebuilt (tower rebuilt 1791)
1769 Colyton. Restored
1779 Exmouth. Rebuilt
1789 Stonehouse, St George. New church. Destroyed second world war
1796 Countisbury. Nave rebuilt
1800 Axminster. South aisle added
1802 Beaford. Tower rebuilt
1810 c Landcross. Projecting, slate-hung bell-turret
1811 Shute. North aisle added
1812 Exeter, St Sidwell. Rebuilt. (Destroyed in second world war and since rebuilt)
1815 Bishopsteignton. West tower built

Eighteenth-century tympana, i e, a solid wall above the screen to fill the chancel arch, are preserved at Molland, Parracombe and Satterleigh.

It is worth noting that while eighteenth-century improvements all came out of the church rate, which the ratepayers of the parish voted themselves, private donors also contributed many church fittings, e g, chandeliers.

2. VICTORIAN

The British nation, after a lapse of some 300 years, now regained interest in their churches. The apathy of the previous century had departed; new churches were built in the rapidly growing cities and towns and a great many old ones were restored—in Devon, only about ten came through the period unscathed. Again, as in the seventeenth century, much of it was necessary only because of the neglect that had gone before. The architect, too, came of age and architecture became national rather than regional. Local characteristics disappeared, the clerestory was accepted (to let in more light), the crypt, or churchroom beneath the building, was introduced for parochial purposes.

Gothic, especially Perpendicular, had never been really abandoned and early in the nineteenth century, in churchbuilding at least, it quickly became the vogue. The Gothic revival, satisfying romantic tastes, worked backwards. The first to regain popularity was the Perpendicular style, then the

Tedburn St Mary: sundial.
Typical of those erected during the
nineteenth century

Decorated, and finally the Early English, the most successful revival of them all. Here and there, as at Honiton and Lynton, attempts were made to imitate the builders from Normandy.

Ide, by Hooper and Cornish, and Stoke Canon by Mason, are typical Devon churches of the 1830s. Added to their old sandstone towers—the original tower was often retained—they look typically medieval from the outside, but are in fact aisleless and uninspiring. How very different is St Paul, Honiton, designed only two years later by Charles Fowler, in the Norman style, with Norman columns and a clerestory—yet with a west tower. It is well built and a credit to its architect, who also designed Bickleigh, near Plymouth (1838), Exeter's Higher Market and the old Lower Market, together with London's Covent Garden market.

Fowler, a man of bold and original ideas, was probably less successful with his roof designs. At Honiton, he used cast iron—then a new material—without considering the possible effects of expansion and contraction. When these caused structural movements, with resultant leaks, he was successfully sued for professional negligence. Later a timber roof was built over the original and very recently the two roofs have been removed and a new one erected.

In the 1840s, more churches were built in Devon than in any other decade of its entire history. At least thirty-two were either under construction or being wholly rebuilt, many of them by Hayward, Devon's most prolific Victorian designer. These churches were being built not only in the towns, but in such isolated places as Twitchen on Exmoor,

Dawlish, St Gregory the Great: Another design by the county's own architect, Andrew Patey, 1824

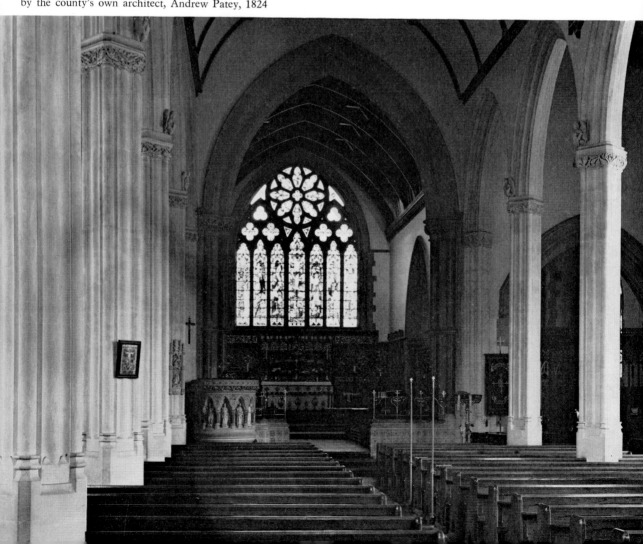

Landscove: by J. L. Pearson,
designer of Truro Cathedral, 1849

East Woolfardisworthy, Bere Alston and Alfington —the last by Butterfield, of brick in the Early English style, with a western bell-turret. All this activity was, to a great degree, due to the untiring efforts of Henry Phillpots, that eager bishop who 'stormed through his diocese to reform abuses and reinvigorate the Church'. In the Three Towns— Plymouth, Devonport and Stonehouse—nine new parishes were formed in seven years under Sir Robert Peel's New Parishes Act. Each parish had its own church and these soon became known as the 'Peel Churches'.

None of these new churches of the bustling seaport—all badly damaged during the second world war—could be called exciting or even particularly good examples of neo-Gothic. Vastly more interesting was the reconstruction at Exeter of St Michael, Heavitree (1844-6), where a large nave was built— the old extended eastwards—so preserving the old Perpendicular columns with their richly carved capitals (arcades and roof raised). Writing in 1842, Spreat complains of St Michael's being far too small to contain the increased population—hardly surprising for such an ancient foundation which was annexed to the cathedral by Pope Eugenius III in 1152. Its crowning glory is the prominent west tower added in 1887, the finest nineteenth-century Perpendicular tower in the diocese. Designed by

Harbertonford: an unusual Victorian church, architect unknown, 1860

E. H. Harbottle, the buttresses are set square and ornamented with tabernacles on each set-off. The parapet table is open, with gargoyles below the string course and eight crocketed pinnacles. On the north, a turret rises above the parapet table and is surmounted by a small spire ornamented with crockets. The chancel was added in 1893.

The altogether exceptional St Bartholomew's at Yealmpton was rebuilt in the Decorated style in 1850 by William Butterfield, an architect keen on local materials and addicted to dazzling interiors of brick, marble, glass and mosaics of varying colours. The exterior is not particularly outstanding but inside are impressive octagonal piers of marble in two shades of grey. The chancel arch incorporates another arch slightly lower and the space between the two is filled with a multi-coloured diaper pattern. John Betjeman has called it 'the most amazing Victorian church in Devon'. Certainly it is a refreshing piece of Victoriana by comparison with the dull interiors of the new Bicton (1851) and Ilfracombe, St Philip and St James (1856), both by Hayward. The tower was added in 1915.

Church-building continued on a large scale throughout the 1860s and important additions included St John, Torquay; Tavistock, St Mary Magdalene; and St Michael and All Angels, Exeter. Meanwhile, restoration of existing structures was continuing at an even greater pace. The cry was often for 'all things new', and in many places the Church Commissioners, the clergy, and the church-wardens gave little thought to design and colour, to heritage and local characteristics, or even to the medieval treasures which remained. In Devon, predominantly rural and virtually untouched by the Industrial Revolution and its ensuing wealth, it is remarkable that so much was saved; without re-building, so much more would have perished.

The situation at Diptford, where the chancel had been destroyed and the aisle windows were in very poor condition—'the piers on both sides are much out of the perpendicular'—was repeated all over the diocese. Edward Ashworth was engaged for the restoration of St Peter, Tiverton (1853-7), and the Reverend J. B. Hughes, describing the old interior, wrote :

'There was no kind of abomination, no description of deformity, no element of un-becomingness, so to speak, which had not been with surprising skill, introduced into the church. A heavy gallery over the chancel successfully drowned the voice of the officiating priest; another in the north aisle spread a

dim, but certainly not a religious light; and a fourth blocked up the tower arch and window. The font was hidden among the high pews which crowded the nave, and the lofty boxes in the chancel concealed the worm-eaten and uncared-for altar. The structure was by no means safe for the walls had fallen outwards many inches, the piers had followed them and the east window had been blocked up with woodwork to ensure that it didn't collapse altogether.'

Unnecessary destruction in the course of re-building occasionally included structural work, as was the case at Chittlehampton (restored 1871-2), where a new young vicar, aided and abetted by his patron, had the north wall, with square-headed windows—offensive in the eyes of the purists—torn down and rebuilt with windows of 'correct' tracery.

Torquay, like Plymouth, was also growing rapidly at this time and no less than ten churches were constructed between 1846 and 1896. The finest is St John, built in 1861, mainly of Devon marble, on the site of the old St John's chapel. The design is by George Edmund Street and the high decorative chancel arch and steps, with delicate brass screen at the approach to the wide chancel, is typical of his work. The spaciousness and height of the interior are particularly impressive and it is said that his inspiration was All Saints, Margaret Street, where he worshipped when in London. The unusual tower of saddleback design, by A. E. Street, was added in 1884 and copied from a church in Normandy. Also of special interest are the large mosaic panels by Salviati of Venice, the exceptionally fine organ of 1873, and the immersion font for adult baptisms—one of only fifteen in the parish churches of England.

St Mary Magdalene at Tavistock (now Roman Catholic) was originally the Fitzford chapel of ease. Given by the Duke of Bedford in 1865 and designed by Henry Clutton, it is neo-Transitional, with a tall and pointed tower at the north-west. Almost Lombardo-Venetian, it is conspicuous and lofty, outshining in many respects its medieval 'mother-church' to the north. The fortunes of the Bedford family were founded upon the Victorian mining boom of the Tavy and Tamar valleys, so that this is yet another example of industrial wealth being bestowed upon a great new Christian edifice. Exeter, St Michael and All Angels (1867-8), was designed by Major Rhode Hawkins in the Early English style. It is of limestone with freestone mouldings, and has a clerestory and a particularly fine west doorway. The three-stage tower has an open parapet table, pinnacles, and a spire rising 220 ft above the city rooftops. Its construction was made possible by a gift of £20,000 from William Gibbs, a merchant of London but by parentage and affection a man of Devon.

Bishop Temple was instrumental in forming sixteen daughter parishes, half of these in the Three Towns, and in the forty years up to 1890, some £80,000 was spent on church-building and restoration in Plymouth alone. Emmanuel, costing £3,000, was erected in 1870 by Reid in the Decorated style. It was extended in 1881 by Hine and Odgers, the steeple being added sixteen years later.

St Mathias (1887), one of eleven new churches in Devon consecrated by Bishop Bickersteth and also the work of Hine and Odgers, has a square Perpendicular tower with large bell-openings. Victorian stained glass, so much of which is gaudy and inferior to that of the fifteenth century, can be seen at its best at St Michael, Torquay (1877).

The late nineteenth century produced three outstanding Devon churches by three different architects, all totally unlike each other in either style or construction. All are in the south for, with the exception of Barnstaple and Ilfracombe, the north did not enjoy the same prosperity nor attract such great increases in population. The first, at Darting-

Torquay, St John: 1861, by G. E. Street.
Tower 1884, by A. E. Street. A beautiful site

ton, was completed in 1880 and was the work of J. L. Pearson, the designer of Truro Cathedral, of whom it has been said that his mastery of Gothic ranked with that of the medieval master-mason. The exact dimensions and style of the old building were skilfully followed, the font, pulpit, south porch, and chancel screen all being re-used. The tower is topped by traceried battlements and pinnacles.

The second, Exeter, St David (1897-1900), was Caroë's finest achievement and is certainly the best-built church in the long history of the city, outside the cathedral. So that the graveyard should be left undisturbed, the contract stipulated that the building was not to exceed the foundations of the second church, which explains the position of buttresses and tower supports. The buttresses are actually placed within, and pierced, thus making the ambulatory aisle round the broad nave, an unusual and striking feature. The west end, complete with a stone screen and flying buttresses, is flanked with two small turrets embattled and spired. The north-east tower is fanciful, with pierced belfry lights and a turret on the west side, a plain parapet table and a dwarf roof.

The third outstanding Devon church of the late

Tavistock, St Mary Magdalene: 1865, by Henry Clutton, with an internal height greater than that of the cathedral at Exeter. Now Roman Catholic

nineteenth century, Shaldon, St Peter, is of red sandstone with polyphant dressings, and was completed 1902. An excellent example of its date, it was designed by E. Sedding, who was much influenced by his brother, J. D. Sedding. A first step away from the period imitation of the nineteenth century, it is unique in several respects. Like a 'tunnel of stone', it has a stone wagon roof and a stone apse, with a stone altar. Illumination is afforded by a large west window and a clerestory held high on tall octagonal piers of greenish polyphant stone. The pulpit is of marble with alabaster steps, and the stone roodscreen of three bays is the finest of its kind in the West Country. Above the open tracery and the cornice stand the figures of St Peter, St John, St Paul, St Nicholas and the Blessed Virgin. Behind St Peter rises the rood with the figure of Our Lord.

Babbacombe, All Saints: 1884-90,
by Butterfield. Typical late Victorian parish church

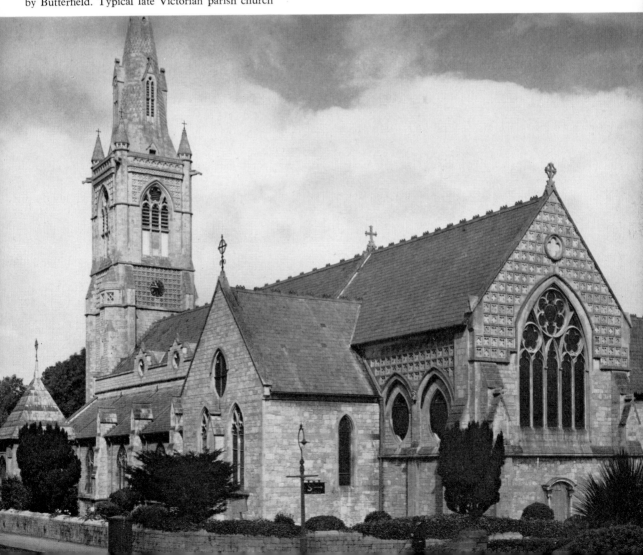

NEW OR WHOLLY REBUILT CHURCHES

The architect, where known, is mentioned in italics. An asterisk indicates the incorporation of an old tower.

1820s. Brixham, All Saints; Dawlish, St Gregory*—*Patey*; East Teignmouth—*Patey*; Exeter, Holy Trinity—*Kendall*; Exmouth; Plymouth, St Catherine—*Foulston*; Plymouth, St Luke; Torquay, St John (chapel); West Teignmouth*—*Patey*.

1830s. Appledore—*Williams*; Bickleigh (Plymouth)—*Fowler*; Blackborough; Bridgetown (Totnes); Chittlehamholt; Cofton; Exeter, Bedford Chapel; Exeter, St Edmund-on-the-Bridge (old materials re-used); Hartland, St John; Honiton, St Paul—*Fowler*; Ide*—*Hooper* and *Cornish*; Meshaw*—*Gould*; Newton Abbot, St Leonard; Oakford*—*Pope*; Plymouth, St Paul; Puddington—*Bowden*; Strete*—*Lidstone*; Stoke Canon*—*Mason*.

1840s. Alfington—*Butterfield*; Arlington—*Gould* (tower 1899); Barnstaple, Newport; Barnstaple, St Mary Magdalene—*Ferrey*; Bere Alston; Chudleigh Knighton—*Scott* and *Moffatt*; Crownhill; Dawlish, St Mark—*Hayward*; East Woolfardisworthy—*Hayward*; Exeter, Heavitree, St Michael; Holcombe Burnell—*Hayward*; Kingswear—*Hayward*; Landscove—*Pearson*; Modbury, St Mary, Brownstone; Okehampton* — *Hayward*; Plymouth, Christ Church; St James the Great (Stoke Damerel); St James the Less; St Mary (Stoke Damerel); St Paul (Stoke Damerel); St Peter—chancel by *Street* (rest 1880-2 by *Fellowes Prynne*, tower 1906); St Stephen (Stoke Damerel)—*Hayward*; Salcombe*—*Ball* (chancel — *Sedding*); Sowton — *Hayward*; Sutton-on-Plym; Tawstock, Harracott; Torquay, St Mary Magdalene—*Salvin* (altered by Scott 1882); Twitchen*—*Hayward*; Westhill; Whimple*—*Hayward*; Withleigh—*Hayward*.

1850s. Ashford—*Gould*; Babbacombe, St Marychurch*—*Hugall*; Bicton—*Hayward*; Bovey Tracey St John; Brampford Speke*; Brentor, Christ Church; Creacombe; Ilfracombe, St Philip & St James—*Hayward*; Monk Okehampton* *Harper* & *Arnold* (east window exhibited Crystal Palace 1851); Oreston; Plymouth, Holy Trinity; Tiverton—St Paul; Torquay, St Mark—*Salvin* (screens—*J. D. Sedding*); Virginstow; Yealmpton*—*Butterfield* (tower 1915).

1860s. Babbacombe, All Saints—*Butterfield*; Barn-

staple, Holy Trinity—*White*; Bideford, St Mary—*Ashworth*; Dawlish, Holcombe; Exeter, St Mary Major—*Ashworth*; Exeter, St Michael & All Angels—*Rhode Hawkins*; Harbertonford; Kilmington*—*Bury*; Lympstone*; Monkton—*Hayward*; Newton Abbot, St Paul—*Rowell*; Petersmarland*; Postbridge; Romansleigh*—*Ashworth*; St Giles-in-the-Wood*; Sidford*—*White*; Sidmouth*; Tavistock, St Mary Magdalene—*Clutton*; Topsham*; Torquay, St John—*Street*; Torquay, St Luke—*Blomfield*; Uplowman*; Uplyme*; West Buckland*—*Gould*.

1870s. Avonwick—*Fulford*; Beer—*Hayward*; Bigbury*—*J. D. Sedding*; Charles; East Anstey*; Exeter, St James—*Fulford*; Halwell*; Huish*; Huxham — *Hayward*; Lamerton*; Otterton*—*Ferrey*; Petrockstow*—*Gould*; Plymouth, All Saints—*Hine* (completed 1910); Plymouth, Emmanuel—*Reid* (extended 1881—*Hine* and *Odgers*, steeple 1897—*Rogers*); Rousdon—*George* and *Vaughan*; Thelbridge; Torquay, St Michael—*Pritchard*.

1880s. Budleigh Salterton—*Fellowes Prynne*; Dartington—*Pearson*; Exeter, St Leonard—*Fulford*; Exeter, St Matthew—*Fulford*; Harpford; Plymouth, St Mathias—*Hine* and *Odgers*; Rockbeare*; Rose Ash*—*St Aubyn* and *Wadling*; Sheepwash—*Gould* (tower by *Webb*); Torquay, All Saints—*Pearson*; Washford Pyne—*Fulford*.

1890s. Exeter, St David—*Caroë*; Horrabridge; Lundy; Lynton*—*J. D. Sedding*; Shaldon, St Peter—*E. Sedding*; Torquay, St Matthew—*Nicholson* and *Corlette*.

1900s. Exmouth, Holy Trinity—*Fellowes Prynne*; Ilfracombe, St Peter—*Fellowes Prynne*; Newton Abbot, St Mary Abbotsbury—*E. Sedding*; Plymouth, St Gabriel—*Caroë*.

EXTENSIONS AND PARTIAL REBUILDING

(Principal work in brackets. Architect where known in italics.)

1820s. Exeter, St Thomas (north aisle); Lympstone (chancel); Sidmouth (south aisle); Southleigh (south aisle); Totnes (outer north aisle)—enlarged 1869.

1830s. Highampton (chancel); Upton Pyne (north aisle).

1840s. Countisbury (north aisle); Dunsford (chancel); Uffculme (outer south aisle).

1850s. Bovey Tracey (outer north aisle); Clannaborough (nave); Clyst Hydon (north aisle); Southleigh (chancel).

1860s. Bishops Tawton (chancel); Bow (chancel); Chudleigh (heavily restored except tower); Churston Ferrers (exterior); Cofton (north aisle); Egg Buckland (chancel and north aisle); Hawkchurch (exterior renewed); Kingsteignton (exterior); Lynton—*Dolby;* Martinhoe (north aisle); Newton Tracey (north aisle)—*Gould;* Powderham (chancel); Silverton (chancel, two west bays and vestry) —*Hayward* and *Ashworth;* South Molton (clerestory); Stoke-in-Teignhead (chancel); Tedburn St Mary (chancel); Trentishoe (chancel).

1870s. Huntsham (north aisle); Kentisbury (north aisle and chancel); Poltimore (south aisle)— *Fulford;* Shobrooke (south aisle); Stowford (north aisle)—*Scott.*

1880s. Brixham, All Saints (south aisle); Dodbrooke (north aisle); East Teignmouth (tower)—*Fulford;* Exeter, Heavitree, St Michael (tower)—*Harbottle;* Exeter, St Petrock (chancel); Holsworthy (chancel and north aisle); Stoodleigh (chancel and chancel aisle); Torquay, St John (tower)—*Street.*

1890s. Brixham, All Saints (north aisle and west front)—*Clarke* (tower and Lady chapel 1900-6 by *Micklethwaite*); Exeter, Heavitree, St Michael (chancel); Highweek (east end); Lydford (north aisle); Mary Tavy (south transept, chancel and chapel lengthened); Milton Damerel (tower); Sutcombe (tower).

Restorations were so numerous that space does not permit them to be listed.

Yealmpton: 1850, by William Butterfield.
Tower added 1915

12. The Twentieth Century

Twentieth-century churchbuilding in Britain gives the impression of being in a transitional period, during which style and shape are changing only as a result of influences from outside rather than from within the Church. Whilst architecture must of necessity be related to theology—as was realized by some of the nineteenth-century ecclesiologists—there is still the feeling that 'a church should look like a church'. In post-war Plymouth, for example, a great opportunity was lost for providing church-goers with imaginative buildings.

Reinforced concrete, invented 150 years ago, was considered too crude to be seen until the 1920s, as was steel. Only since the second world war have these materials been used to any extent in church-building. Why, one wonders, do so many find it

Buckfast Abbey: 1907-32. Tower completed 1938, mainly to the design of F. A. Walters

Milber, Newton Abbot: twentieth-century
church architecture at its finest

acceptable for a college of education to be built of steel and glass, but not an ecclesiastical building? Other European countries have been much more adventurous than Britain, as evidenced by the work of such world-famous architects as Rudolf Schwarz, Emil Steffann and Andre Le Donné.

In Devon, Caroë, after his success with Exeter, St David, failed with Plymouth, St Gabriel (1908), Plymouth, St Mary, and Woolacombe (1911). The last, in red sandstone, though the best of the three, is still small and unimpressive compared with churches built fifty years earlier. Woolbrook, Sid-mouth (1938), Caroë's last work, is little better, the only redeeming feature being the east window by Cooper-Abbs, which was erected in 1958. The only pre-1939 church to approach the best of the nineteenth century is Yelverton (1913), by Nichol-son and Corlette. Though still bound by tradition, with wagon roofs and tall arcades of Ham Hill stone, its colourful roof decoration—red and green in nave and aisles, red and blue in chancel, with black and white chequer work—imparts a fresh-ness and widely contrasts with the roofs of the Victorian era.

Crownhill: a unique altar is the centrepiece of this post-war church

The second world war, and the shift in population to new areas, resulted in the building of many new churches, and never before has there been such extreme divergence in design. The Church of England alone has built well over 300 new churches in the past twenty years and the Exeter diocese has been one of the most active. The finest of the new Devon churches, however, was conceived between the wars, on the new housing estate at Milber, Newton Abbot. Of unusual design, with three naves radiating from the sanctuary and linked together by double arcades, it is unique in that the width, length, and total height from the foundations, are the same (83 ft 4 in, or 1,000 in). Building started in 1936 and, after suspension during the war years, the church was finally completed and consecrated in 1963. The total cost was estimated at £48,750.

Another new church which is also the centrepiece of a new housing development—the Church of the Ascension, Crownhill (1956)—has received even more attention than Milber. With a tower foreign to Devon, though by no means out of place in its setting, it is traditional in that it retains the rectangular nave. The altar is brought westward into the midst of the congregation and impressively backed at the east end by a unique wall, designed by Geoffrey Clarke, of roughly hewn granite, and glass in shades of blue, amber, green and red. The only church in the diocese, apart from Milber, which can be labelled twentieth century, it has smooth, slim granite pillars supporting a maroon-coloured roof of reinforced concrete. The overall impression of simplicity and asceticism is somewhat spoilt by white-painted pews of poor design.

St James the Less at West Hoe, Plymouth, which was destroyed by bombing, was rebuilt in 1958 in a new housing area at Ham. Designed by Evans and Sloggett, it is rectangular in plan, with a structural steel frame externally faced by brickwork. It has a fine east window by Sir Ninian Comper, and a church-hall at the west provides one of the amenities required by a modern community centre. At Exeter, the post-war St Sidwell's (1957) occupies the site of the original church and beneath it is the traditional tomb of its founder-saint—a place of pilgrimage for some 1,400 years. By Lucas, Roberts and Brown, the interior construction involved the casting in situ of massive reinforced concrete arches; the one over the sanctuary entrance being the largest ever cast up to that time. The east end is distinguished by a large mural by Hans Feibusch, while the west end has a window, by Pattison of Bideford, depicting the martyrdom of St Sidwell, and a representation of the old church being destroyed by two enemy aircraft.

What does the future hold for the churches of Devon, particularly the village church with its medieval heritage? One of the great paradoxes of modern times is the decline in church-going coupled with a genuine interest in religion itself. Will some churches perish, or become musty museums? Or will they gain renewed vigour in a Britain more aware of its great debt to Christianity? Sufficient perhaps to quote recent instances of some small churches in the backwaters of north Devon; if these are typical examples, then surely there is little to fear.

CHITTLEHAMHOLT. Population 200. In 1960 in a deplorable state externally and internally. Now restored inside and out, and fitted with electric light, oil-fired heating and new organ.

FILLEIGH. Population 200. In 1963 no service from Christmas Day until Easter, the rector being ill and the churchwarden and his wife comprising the sole congregation. Now one of the most flourishing. Recent tower repairs cost nearly £1,000, all raised in the parish.

GEORGE NYMPTON. Population 120. Some ten years ago the incumbent forecast its closure in view of the heavy cost of repair, whereupon it was splendidly restored by the parishioners.

SATTERLEIGH. Population 20. In 1946 unused, with brambles growing everywhere and ash saplings overtopping the north wall. Now beautifully restored and with a regular Sunday service.

WARKLEIGH. Population 100. In 1956 a monthly service was attended by the rector's wife and two other people. There was a hole in the floor, others in the roof, the organ was decayed and the churchyard a mass of bramble. Now in regular use, it has been restored, together with its six bells. It is also the proud possessor of a ciborium—a container for the consecrated bread—with decorated sides coloured in green, red, white and gold, and of a kind very rare, if not unique, in England.

CHURCHES DESTROYED DURING THE SECOND WORLD WAR

Aveton Giffard :	rebuilt on same site
Clyst St George :	rebuilt on same site
Exeter —	
Bedford :	
St James :	rebuilt on new site
St Lawrence :	
St Sidwell :	rebuilt on same site
Plymouth —	

St Andrew :	rebuilt on same site
St George (Stonehouse) :	
St James the Great (Devonport) :	severely damaged, later demolished
St James the Less :	rebuilt at Ham
St Michael (Devonport) :	rebuilt on same site
St Paul (Devonport) :	
St Peter :	rebuilt on same site
St Saviour and Holy Trinity :	
St Stephen (Devonport) :	
Torquay — St Marychurch :	rebuilt on same site

POST-WAR CHURCHES IN NEW HOUSING AREAS

Exeter
St Andrew (daughter church, parish of St Thomas)
St Boniface, Whipton
St Lawrence (daughter church, parish of Heavitree)
St Paul, Burnthouse Lane
Plymouth
The Church of the Ascension, Crownhill
St Aidan, Ernesettle
St Chad, Whitleigh
Torquay
New church in the Sherwell Valley (daughter church, parish of Cockington)

The 1967 edition of the *Church of England Year Book* records 535 parish churches in the Diocese of Exeter.

Crownhill: a handsome Christian edifice on the outskirts of the new Plymouth

APPENDIXES

1: BENCH ENDS

Fifteenth Century

Ashton
Atherington
Braunton (bench fronts)
Cheldon
Colebrooke
Cookbury

Dowland
Ilsington
Nymet Rowland
Plymtree
Rewe

Thorverton
Upton Hellions
Virginstow
Welcombe
Westleigh

Sixteenth Century

Abbotsham
Alwington
Ashwater
Bere Ferrers
Bickleigh (near Tiverton)
Bradford
Braunton
Broadhempston
Broadwoodwidger
Buckland Brewer
Buckland Monachorum
Cheriton Bishop
Christow
Chudleigh
Clayhanger
Cockington
Colaton Raleigh
Coldridge
Combe-in-Teignhead
Combe Martin
Countisbury
Doddiscombsleigh
  (made into choir stalls)
Down St Mary
Dunchideock

East Budleigh
Feniton
Frithelstock
Great Torrington
Harpford
Hartland
Hatherleigh
High Bickington
Holcombe Rogus
Honeychurch
Horwood
Kenn
Landcross
Lapford
Lewtrenchard
Lifton
Marwood
Monkleigh
Mortehoe
Newton St Petrock
North Bovey
Northleigh
Northlew
North Tawton
Ottery St Mary

Parracombe
Payhembury
Plympton St Mary
Powderham
Puddington
St Giles-on-the-Heath
Sandford
Satterleigh
Shillingford
South Tawton
Stockleigh Pomeroy
Sutcombe
Swimbridge
Talaton
Tawstock
Tedburn St Mary
Tetcott
Thornbury (made into choir stalls)
Warkleigh
Weare Giffard
West Putford
West Worlington
Woodbury
Woolsery
Yarcombe

Seventeenth Century

Ashcombe
Clovelly
Clyst St Lawrence

Hatherleigh (box pew)
Hittisleigh (squire's pew)
Holcombe Rogus (Bluett pew)

Shobrooke
Totnes (Corporation pews)

Eighteenth Century (box pews unless otherwise stated)

Buckerell
Clyst Hydon
Cruwys Morchard
Dowland
Gittisham

Kings Nympton
Knowstone (bench ends)
Littleham, nr Bideford
  (bench ends)
Molland

Parracombe
Poltimore (squire's pew)
Torbryan (box pews covering
  original benches)

Early nineteenth-century box pews are to be seen at Halwell and Holcombe Burnell

Modern (notable carving)

Black Torrington
Crediton
Dunchideock
Ermington
Exbourne
High Bickington (choir stalls)

Holbeton (choir stalls)
Kingswear
Lydford
Poltimore
Rose Ash
Sheepstor

Tavistock, St Eustace (chiefly
  copies of original)
Venn Ottery
Yelverton

2: BRASSES
Churches which contain dated brasses in a good or reasonable condition

Ashburton
Ashton
Atherington
Berry Pomeroy
Bickleigh
Bigbury
Blackawton
Charles
Chittlehampton
Clovelly
Cockington
Colyton
Combe-in-Teignhead
Combe Martin
Dartmouth, St Petrock
Dartmouth, St Saviour
Diptford
Doddiscombsleigh
East Allington
Ermington

Exminster
Farway
Filleigh
Haccombe
Harford
Hartland
Heanton Punchardon
Kentisbeare
Lewtrenchard
Lifton
Loxhore
Lympstone
Marwood
Monkleigh
Okehampton
Otterdon
Ottery St Mary
Petrockstowe
Pilton
Plymouth, St Andrew

St Giles-in-the-Wood
Sandford
Shillingford
Sidbury
Staverton
Stoke Fleming
Stoke-in-Teignhead
Sydenham Damerel
Tedburn St Mary
Tiverton, St Peter
Torquay, St Saviour
Trusham
Ugborough
Washfield
Wembury
West Alvington
Woodland
Yealmpton

3: CAPITALS (figure and foliage)

Abbotskerswell
Alphington
Ashcombe
Berrynarbor
Berry Pomeroy
Bishopsteignton
Bovey Tracey
Bradninch
Broadclyst
Broadhembury
Broadhempston
Broadwoodwidger
Calverleigh
Cheriton Fitzpaine
Churston Ferrers
Cockington
Coffinswell
Combe Martin
Crediton

Cruwys Morchard
Cullompton
Dartmouth, St Saviour
Doddiscombsleigh
Dunsford
East Ogwell
Exeter, Heavitree, St Michael
Gittisham
Harberton
Hawkchurch
Holcombe Rogus
Kenton
Kingskerswell
Kingsteignton
Lifton
Little Hempston
Marldon
Molland
Northleigh

Ottery St Mary
Payhembury
Pinhoe
Powderham
Sampford Courtenay
Sandford
South Molton
Stockleigh Pomeroy
Stoke Gabriel
Stoke-in-Teignhead
Sutcombe
Swimbridge
Thorverton
Tiverton, St Peter
Torbryan
West Alvington
West Worlington
Wolborough

4: CELURES

Hatherleigh (one bay only)
Hennock
Ideford

Ilfracombe, Holy Trinity
Kings Nympton
Lapford

Satterleigh
Swimbridge
Talaton

5: CHANDELIERS

Ashburton
Axminster
Braunton
Chulmleigh
Colyton

Cornworthy
Culmstock
Dartmouth, St Saviour
Hatherleigh
Hemyock

Lewtrenchard
Tiverton, St Peter
Totnes
Uffculme

6: CHESTS

Ashburton (1483)
Ashwater (Jacobean)
Bradford (medieval)
Bradninch (1679)
Braunton (*c* 1580)
Cadbury (medieval)
Calverleigh (Jacobean)
Colebrooke (Jacobean)
Combe Martin (*c* 1560)
Crediton (*c* 1420)
Cullompton (medieval)
Frithelstock (medieval)

Loxbeare (seventeenth century)
Northlew (medieval)
Sampford Courtenay (medieval)
Silverton (Jacobean)
South Molton (Jacobean)
Swimbridge (Jacobean)
Tavistock, St Eustace (fourteenth century)
Warkleigh (medieval)
West Worlington (seventeenth century)
Winkleigh (Jacobean)
Yarnscombe (fourteenth century)

7: CLERESTORIES

Axminster
Colyton
Crediton
Cullompton
Culmstock

Hawkchurch
Honiton, St Paul
North Molton
Poltimore
Pyworthy

Sandford
South Molton
Tiverton, St Peter

8: DOORWAYS—Norman

Axminster
Axmouth
Bickleigh (nr Tiverton)
Bishopsteignton
Bondleigh
Bow
Bradford
Bradstone

Brushford
Buckland Brewer
Buckland Filleigh
Dowland
East Worlington
Highampton
High Bickington
Holcombe Burnell

Hollacombe
Knowstone
Lapford
Loxbeare
Marystow
Meeth
Mortehoe
Northleigh

Northlew
Nymet Rowland
Paignton
Parkham
Salcombe Regis
Shebbear

Shobrooke
Southleigh
South Milton
Stockleigh Pomeroy
Sutcombe
Thornbury

Tiverton, St Peter
Upton Hellions
Whitchurch
Woolsery

9: EASTER SEPULCHRES

Bere Ferrers
Holcombe Burnell
Ottery St Mary

South Pool
Throwleigh

West Alvington
Woodleigh

10: FONTS

Norman

Abbotsham
Alphington
Alverdiscott
Ashford
Ashprington
Ashwater
Beaford
Bere Ferrers
Berrynarbor
Bickleigh (near Tiverton)
Bideford
Bishops Nympton
Bishops Tawton (Jacobean cover)
Blackawton
Bishopsteignton
Bondleigh
Bradford
Bradworthy
Bratton Clovelly
Braunton
Brendon
Bridgerule
Broadwoodwidger
Buckfastleigh (Jacobean cover)
Buckland-in-the-Moor
Buckland Monachorum
Burrington
Butterleigh
Cadbury
Cheriton Bishop
Christow
Chudleigh
Churchstow
Clawton

Clayhanger
Clovelly
Clyst Honiton
Clyst St Lawrence
Coffinswell
Colaton Raleigh
Coldridge
Combe-in-Teignhead
Cookbury
Cornworthy
Crediton (modern cover)
Dartmouth, St Petrock
Dean Prior
Denbury
Dittisham
Dodbrooke
Dolton
Down St Mary
Dunkeswell
East Putford
Eggesford
Ermington
Exeter, St Mary Steps
Exeter, St Pancras
Farringdon
Frithelstock
Halberton
Harberton
Hartland
Hatherleigh (eighteenth-century
 cover)
Highampton
High Bickington
High Bray

Hittisleigh
Holbeton
Hollacombe
Honeychurch
Horwood
Huxham
Ilfracombe, Holy Trinity
Instow
Inwardleigh
Jacobstow
Kenn
Landcross
Lifton
Loddiswell
Luffincott
Luppitt
Lustleigh
Lydford
Malborough
Mariansleigh
Marystow
Meeth
Merton (Jacobean cover)
Molland
Monkleigh
Morleigh
Northlew
Netherexe
Newton St Petrock
Newton Tracey
Northleigh
Nymet Rowland
Paignton
Pancrasweek

Parkham
Parracombe
Petrockstow (Jacobean cover)
Pinhoe
Plymstock (sixteenth-century cover)
Poltimore
Rattery
Sampford Courtenay
Sampford Peverell
St Giles-on-the-Heath
Shaldon, St Nicholas
Sheepwash
Sheldon
Shirwell

South Brent
South Milton
South Pool
Spreyton
Stoke Canon
Stoke Fleming
Stokenham
Talaton
Tetcott
Thurlestone
Topsham
Torquay, St Marychurch
Trusham
Twitchen

Ugborough (seventeenth-century cover)
Upton Hellions
Virginstow
Washfield
Weare Giffard
West Anstey
West Down
West Putford
Wolborough
Woodleigh
Woolsery
Yealmpton
Zeal Monachorum

Early Gothic

Aveton Giffard
Black Torrington
Brixham, St Mary
Calverleigh
Challacombe
Combe Martin
Dartmouth, St Clement

Dunchideock
East Ogwell
Feniton
Hennock
Kingsbridge
Kingswear
Landkey

Littleham (near Exmouth)
Little Hempston
Little Torrington (Jacobean cover)
Northam
Pilton (Tudor cover, sixteenth-century canopy)

Perpendicular

Abbotskerswell
Ashton
Bovey Tracey
Bow
Branscombe
Broadhembury
Broadwoodkelly
Chulmleigh
Churston Ferrers
Cockington (Jacobean cover)
Colebrooke (Jacobean cover)
Cotleigh
Countisbury
Highweek
Holcombe Burnell (Jacobean cover)
Iddesleigh (Jacobean cover)
Ideford
Ipplepen

Kingsteignton
Lamerton (Jacobean cover)
Langtree
Loxhore (sixteenth-century cover)
Mamhead
Membury
North Molton
Payhembury
Plympton St Mary
Plymtree
Puddington
Rackenford
Rewe
Rockbeare
Salcombe
Satterleigh
Shaugh Prior (with cover)
Shillingford
Sidbury

South Molton
Sutcombe
Swimbridge (with cover and canopy—early eighteenth-century casing)
Tamerton Foliot
Tavistock, St Eustace
Throwleigh
Torbryan (Jacobean cover)
Totnes
Upottery
Walkhampton
Walkleigh
West Alvington
Witheridge
Woodbury
Yarcombe
Yarnscombe

Post-Reformation

Axmouth
Charles
Exeter, St Thomas
Exminster

Kings Nympton
Martinhoe
Meavy
North Huish

Plympton, St Maurice (with unique early eighteenth-century cover)
Torquay, St John

11: MEDIEVAL GLASS
Asterisk signifies considerable remains; otherwise fragments only

Abbots Bickington
Ashton*
Atherington*
Bere Ferrers
Berry Pomeroy
Bondleigh
Branscombe
Bridford
Broadwoodkelly*
Cadbury
Cockington
Coldridge
Doddiscombsleigh*
East Ogwell
Exeter Cathedral*
Gidleigh
Gittisham
Haccombe

Hennock
Highweek
Holcombe Burnell
Horwood
Huxham
Inwardleigh
Kelly
Kingskerswell
Littleham (near Exmouth)
Lustleigh
Lydford
Manaton
Monkleigh
Northleigh
North Molton
Paignton
Pancrasweek
Petrockstow

Powderham
Salcombe Regis
Sampford Courtenay*
Shillingford
Stockleigh Pomeroy
Sutcombe*
Sydenham Damerel
Tawstock
Torbryan
Upottery
Upton Pyne
Weare Giffard
Whitestone
Winkleigh
Wolborough
Yarcombe
Yarnscombe

12: MEDIEVAL TILES

Abbots Bickington
Alverdiscott
Black Torrington
Bradford
Bradworthy
Buckland-in-the-Moor
Cadeleigh
Clawton
Coldridge

Cookbury
East Putford
Haccombe
Horwood
Huntshaw
Instow
Inwardleigh
Milton Damerel
Monkleigh

Newton Tracey
Northlew
Ottery St Mary
Parkham
Sutcombe
Tawstock
Westleigh
West Putford

13: MISERICORDS (medieval)

Bovey Tracey
Cockington

Exeter Cathedral
Kingsbridge

Ottery St Mary

14: MONUMENTS
Churches with notable examples

Pre-Reformation (asterisk denotes also post-Reformation)

Ashwater
Atherington
Axmouth
Bere Ferrers
Berry Pomeroy

Bickleigh (near Plymouth)
Bideford*
Bishops Nympton
Broadclyst*
Coldridge

Colyton*
Crediton*
Exeter Cathedral*
Exeter, St Mary Arches
Feniton

Georgeham
Haccombe★
Heanton Punchardon
Horwood
Iddesleigh

Monkleigh
Morchard Bishop
Mortehoe
Ottery St Mary★
Tamerton Foliot★

Tawstock★
Weare Giffard★
West Down
Widworthy

Post-Reformation

Alverdiscott
Ashton
Barnstaple, St Peter
Berrynarbor
Bicton (mausoleum)
Bishops Tawton
Bovey Tracey
Branscombe
Buckland Monachorum
Burlescombe
Cadeleigh
Calverleigh
Chagford
Dunchideock
Dunsford
East Ogwell

Eggesford
Ermington
Exminster
Gittisham
Holbeton
Holcombe Rogus
Lamerton
Landkey
Lifton
Littleham (near Exmouth)
Littleham (near Bideford)
Marwood
Marystow
Molland
Musbury
Newton St Cyres

North Molton
Pilton
Poltimore
Shute
South Tawton
Tavistock, St Eustace
Tetcott
Thornbury
Tiverton, St Peter
Torquay, St Saviour
Upton Hellions
Wembury
Wolborough
Woolsery

15: PISCINAE

Churches with good examples. Asterisk denotes Norman

Ashton
Axminster
Bere Ferrers
Berrynarbor
Bigbury
Blackawton
Black Torrington
Bradford
Bradworthy
Branscombe
Bridgerule
Brixham, St Mary
Broadhempston
Broadwoodkelly
Buckerell
Buckfastleigh
Burlescombe
Butterleigh
Cheriton Fitzpaine
Churston Ferrers
Clawton★
Coffinswell
Coldridge
Colyton
Crediton

Dartmouth, St Saviour
Denbury
Dunsford
Ermington
Exeter, St Pancras
Harberton
Harford
High Bickington★
Hittisleigh
Horwood
Huxham
Iddesleigh
Ilfracombe, Holy Trinity
Ilsington
Inwardleigh
Kingsbridge
Kingskerswell
Lodiswell
Luppitt★
Lustleigh
Lydford
Malborough
Marldon
Marwood
Membury

Milton Damerel
Netherexe
Newton Ferrers
Northleigh
Paignton (modern)
Petrockstow★
Pilton
Plympton St Mary
Poltimore
Pyworthy
Rockbeare
Rose Ash
Sampford Courtenay
Sampford Peverell
Shebbear
South Brent
South Pool
Spreyton★
Sutcombe
Thornbury
Thurlestone
Trusham★
Upottery
Upton Pyne
West Alvington

West Anstey
West Down
West Worlingham

Wembworthy
Whitchurch
Widworthy

Woodbury

16: PORCHES (of more than usual interest)

Awliscombe
Bere Ferrers
Berry Pomeroy
Brixham, St Mary
Broadwoodwidger
Cheriton Fitzpaine
Churston Ferrers
Colyton
Combe Martin
Crediton
Dartington
Dartmouth, St Saviour
East Ogwell
Ermington
Frithelstock
Harberton
Hartland

Holcombe Rogus
Ilsington
Ipplepen
Kenton
Kingskerswell
Kings Nympton
Lifton
Little Hempston
Malborough
Manaton
Marldon
Marystow
Moretonhampstead
Ottery St Mary
Paignton
Payhembury
Shaugh Prior

Sidbury
Silverton
South Pool (in the middle ages
    contained a rare porch altar)
South Tawton
Staverton
Tawstock
Thorverton
Thurlestone
Tiverton, St Peter
Torbryan
Totnes
Ugborough
Wolborough
Yarcombe

17: PULPITS

Medieval (stone)

Bovey Tracey
Chittlehampton
Dartmouth, St Saviour
Dittisham

Harberton
Paignton
Pilton
South Molton

Swimbridge
Totnes
Witheridge

Medieval (wood). Asterisk denotes inclusion of panels from medieval roodscreen and roodloft

Alverdiscott
Alwington*
Bigbury (brought from
    Ashburton 1777)
Chivelstone
Clayhidon
Cockington
Coldridge
Cullompton

Dartington
East Allington
Halberton
Holne
Ideford*
Ipplepen
Kenton (reconstructed)
Kingsbridge*
North Molton

Pinhoe
Shebbear*
Sherford*
Stoke Gabriel
Throwleigh
Torbryan
Wolborough

Post-Reformation—late sixteenth century

Cheriton Bishop (restored)
Honeychurch
Ilfracombe, Holy Trinity

Sutcombe
Ugborough
Welcombe (restored)

Yarcombe (linenfold panels from
    Buckland Abbey)

Seventeenth Century. Asterisk denotes good Jacobean

Ashton★
Axminster (once three-decker)
Blackawton★
Bow
Bradworthy★
Braunton★
Brushford★
Clovelly★
Cookbury★
Cornwood★
Dalwood
Dartmouth, St Petrock

Drewsteignton★
Exbourne
Exeter, St Pancras
Frithelstock★
Great Torrington
Horwood
Iddesleigh
Langtree
Loxbeare
Marwood
Milton Damerel★
Northleigh★

Pancrasweek★
Parkham
Petrockstow★
Plymstock
Satterleigh★
Stoke Canon★
Tamerton Foliot
Uplyme★
West Ogwell
Woodbury★

Eighteenth Century

Branscombe (three-decker)
Cheldon
Churston Ferrers
Cornworthy
Cruwys Morchard
Doddiscombsleigh
Down St Mary
Dunsford
Dunterton
Exeter, St James
Exminster

Hatherleigh (includes some
    screenwork)
Kentisbeare
Landcross (of older bench ends)
Molland (three-decker)
Morchard Bishop (two-decker)
Morleigh
Newton St Cyres
Offwell (two-decker)
Ottery St Mary
Parracombe
Payhembury

Plymtree
Princetown
Salcombe Regis
Sampford Courtenay
South Tawton
Staverton
Stockleigh Pomeroy
    (includes bench fronts)
Uffculme
Upton Hellions
Warkleigh
West Putford

Modern (notable work)

Black Torrington (Jacobean style)
Combe Martin
Crediton
Dawlish
Dunchideock
Haccombe (1822 by Kendall)
Holbeton

Huish
Kings Nympton
Lapford
Lewtrenchard (medieval design)
Loddiswell
Newton St Petrock
Northam

North Bovey (medieval design)
Rose Ash
Tavistock, St Eustace
Tiverton, St Peter
Willand (early nineteenth-century
    two-decker)

18: SCREENS

With original vaulting in situ

Atherington
Bampton
Berry Pomeroy
Bovey Tracey (restored)
Bradninch
Buckerell
Burrington
Chawleigh

Chulmleigh
Clyst St Lawrence
Coldridge (also notable parclose
    screen)
Cullompton
Dartmouth, St Saviour
    (also notable parclose screen)
Feniton

Halberton
Harberton
Hartland
Kentisbeare
Kings Nympton
Lapford
Marwood
Northleigh (part)

Payhembury
Pinhoe
Plymtree
Poltimore

South Pool (part)
Swimbridge
Talaton
Totnes (stone)

Uffculme
Willand

With new vaulting

Ashton
Broadhempston
Buckland-in-the-Moor
Combe-in-Teignhead
Down St Mary
Dunchideock

Heanton Punchardon (part)
Ipplepen
Kenn
Kenton
Lewtrenchard
Lydford (modern screen)

Manaton
Mary Tavy (modern)
Paignton (modern screen)
Plympton St Maurice
  (modern screen)
Staverton (spandrels old)

Early type (c 1380-1410)

Atherington (nave)
Bere Ferrers
Bishops Tawton
Bow
Braunton

Burlescombe
Calverleigh
East Budleigh
East Ogwell
Exbourne (much restored)

Huxham
Stoke-in-Teignhead
Welcombe
Willand

Others—Perpendicular. Asterisk denotes much restored

Abbotskerswell★
Alphington
Awliscombe (early sixteenth-
  century stone)
Blackawton
Bridford
Brushford (parclose screen)
Burlescombe★
Cheriton Bishop (north chancel
  chapel)
Chivelstone
Christow
Chudleigh
Cockington★
Colebrooke (also parclose screen)
Combe Martin (also parclose
  screen)
Cornworthy★
Dartington
Dittisham
Dodbrooke★ (also parclose screen)
East Allington
East Portlemouth
Exeter, St Mary Steps

Exeter, Heavitree, St Michael
  (parclose screen)
Exminster
Feniton★ (also parclose screen)
Gidleigh★
Hennock
Holbeton★
Holne
Honiton, St Michael
  (copy of original)
Ilsington
Kingsbridge (parclose screen)
Littleham★ (near Exmouth)
Little Hempston
Malborough (parclose screens)
Membury
Monkleigh (between aisle and
  Annery chapel)
Morchard Bishop (reconstruction
  of original)
North Bovey
North Huish
Ottery St Mary (parclose screen)
Pilton★ (also parclose screen)

Powderham
Plymstock
Rattery
Rewe
Rose Ash
Sheepstor (reconstruction of
  original)
Sherford
South Milton (also parclose screen)
South Pool
Stoke Gabriel★
Stokenham★
Sutcombe★
Tawstock
Torbryan
Trusham★
Ugborough
Walkleigh
West Worlington (parclose screen)
Widecombe-in-the-Moor
  (wainscoting only)
Wolborough (also parclose screen)
Woodbury★

Post-Reformation

Cheldon
Countisbury
Cruwys Morchard
Ermington

Georgeham
Lustleigh
Molland
Parracombe

Rose Ash (north aisle and
  parclose screen)
Washfield
Whitestone

Modern

Ashburton	Littleham (near Bideford)	Sampford Courtenay (with fragments of original)
Dunsford (stone)	Moretonhampstead	
Haccombe (stone)—1822 by Kendall	Northlew (wainscoting from original)	Shaldon, St Peter
		South Tawton

Notable medieval destroyed in nineteenth century

Ashcombe	Fremington	Poughill
Ashprington	Gittisham	Romansleigh
Bradstone	Halwell	Sampford Courtenay
Bratton Clovelly	Hatherleigh	Sampford Peverell
Bondleigh	High Bickington	Shebbear
Bridestowe	Ide	Sheepstor (reconstructed)
Brixham, St Mary	Ideford	Shirwell
Broadhembury	Kentisbury	South Brent
Bulkworthy	Kingsteignton	South Tawton
Churchstanton	Lewtrenchard (reconstructed)	Tetcott
Clyst Honiton	Loxbeare	Tiverton, St Peter
Dawlish, St Gregory	Marldon (stone)	Wembury
Dean Prior	Monk Okehampton	West Buckland
Doddiscombsleigh	Moretonhampstead	West Ogwell
Dunsford	Plymouth, St Andrew	Whimple

19: ROOFS—Devon's finest

Abbotsham	Coldridge	Lapford
Alverdiscott	Combe Martin	Luffincott
Ashcombe	Cotleigh	Luppitt
Ashwater	Cullompton	Marwood
Beaford	Dartmouth, St Clement	Meavy
Bishops Nympton	Dartmouth, St Petrock	Molland
Black Torrington	Dowland	Morebath
Bondleigh	Dunchideock	Mortehoe
Branscombe	Frithelstock	Northam
Braunton	Gittisham	North Bovey
Bridgerule	Great Torrington	Northlew
Broadclyst	Harberton	Nymet Rowland
Broadhembury	Harford	Ottery St Mary
Buckland Monachorum	Hartland	Pancrasweek
Burlescombe	Hatherleigh	Payhembury
Burrington	Highweek	Pilton
Calverleigh	Hittisleigh	Pyworthy
Chawleigh	Holbeton (modern)	Rackenford
Cheldon	Holcombe Rogus	Sampford Courtenay
Cheriton Bishop	Huntshaw	Sandford
Cheriton Fitzpaine	Ilfracombe, Holy Trinity	Shebbear
Chulmleigh	Ilsington	Shirwell
Churchstow	Kings Nympton	Sidbury
Clawton	Landcross	Silverton
Clyst St Lawrence	Landkey	South Molton

South Pool
South Tawton
Stoodleigh
Stowford
Swimbridge
Sydenham Damerel
Talaton

Tavistock, St Eustace
Tawstock
Throwleigh
Thrushelton
Thurlestone
Ugborough
Upton Hellions

Warkleigh
Weare Giffard
West Down
West Worlingham
Winkleigh
Woodbury

20: SEDILIA

Axminster
Bere Ferrers
Bigbury
Blackawton
Black Torrington
Bradford
Branscombe
Broadclyst
Broadhempston

Buckfastleigh
Crediton
Dartmouth, St Saviour
Harberton
High Bickington
Loddiswell
Lustleigh
Marystow
Newton Ferrers

Ottery St Mary
Paignton (modern)
Plympton, St Mary
Pyworthy
Rewe
Sheepwash
South Brent
West Ogwell

21: SUNDIALS
Dates given where known

Alverdiscott 1823
Bampton 1586
Barnstaple, St Peter 1787
Beaford
Beer
Berrynarbor 1767
Bittadon 1767
Bondleigh 1706
Bradford 1814
Bradworthy
Branscombe
Braunton 1795
Brendon 1707
Bridgerule
Broadwoodkelly
Buckland Brewer 1736
Buckland Filleigh 1727
Chagford
Chawleigh
Clawton 1634
Cheriton Fitzpaine
Clovelly 1678
Colebrooke 1700
Combe Martin 1763
Countisbury
Cruwys Morchard

Diptford 1694
East Down 1709
Ermington 1730
Fremington 1724
Frithelstock 1741
Georgeham 1773
Great Torrington 1832
Harberton 1855
Hatherleigh
Heanton Punchardon 1795
High Bray 1717
Iddesleigh 1720
Ilfracombe, Holy Trinity 1788
Kenn
Kentisbury 1762
Kings Nympton 1846
Lamerton
Landkey 1768
Langtree 1641
Littleham (near Exmouth) 1780
Little Torrington 1771
Loxhore
Marwood 1762
Milton Damerel 1808
Monkleigh
Newton St Cyres 1817

Newton St Petrock 1723
North Molton 1818
North Tawton
Parkham 1731
Parracombe 1726
Pilton 1780
Pyworthy (modern)
Romansleigh 1730
St Giles-in-the-Wood
Sandford 1813
Shebbear
Shirwell 1750
Sidbury
South Molton 1710
Staverton
Stoke Rivers 1770
Stowford 1776
Sutcombe 1785
Swimbridge 1755
Tawstock 1757
Uplowman 1667
Warkleigh
Washford
Winkleigh
Woolsery
Yarnscombe 1788

22: TOWERS

(N—Norman.   D—Decorated.   P—Perpendicular.   V—Victorian.   Asterisk denotes
particularly fine example)

The Best Fifty in Devon

Alwington P	Colyton N/P	Ottery St Mary D
Ashburton P★	Combe Martin P★	Plymouth, St Andrew P
Barnstaple, St Peter D	Crediton P	Plympton St Mary P
Barnstaple, Holy Trinity V	Crownhill (1956)	Sidbury N
Berrynarbor P	Cullompton P★	South Brent N
Bickleigh (near Plymouth) P	Dean Prior D	South Molton P
Bishops Nympton P★	Exeter, Heavitree V	Spreyton P
Branscombe N★	Hartland P★	Talaton P
Braunton N	Hawkchurch P	Tawstock D
Broadclyst P	Holbeton P	Teignmouth, St Michael V
Buckland Brewer P	Ipplepen P	Tiverton, St Peter P
Buckland Monachorum P	Kentisbeare D	Torbryan P
Cheriton Bishop P	Kenton P	Totnes P
Chittlehampton P★	Loxbeare N	Upton Pyne P
Christow (rebuilt 1630)	Modbury D	West Alvington P
Chulmleigh P	Moretonhampstead P	Widecombe-in-the-Moor P
Colebrooke P	North Molton P	

23: TYMPANA—Norman

Bishopsteignton	Down St Mary	Ipplepen
Bondleigh	Ideford	Loxbeare
Chulmleigh		

24: WALL PAINTINGS—Medieval

Ashton	Bratton Clovelly	Littleham (near Bideford)
Branscombe	Clyst St Lawrence	Weare Giffard

(Paintings of the originals can be seen at Bovey Tracey—uncovered at the Victorian
restoration but subsequently lost when exposed to light)

25: WINDOWS

Listing those of more than usual interest, i e tracery, not glass

Aveton Giffard	Cullompton	Plymouth, St Andrew
Axminster	Exbourne	Plympton St Mary
Bere Ferrers	Exeter, St David	South Brent
Bovey Tracey	Exeter, St Martin	Staverton
Bradninch	Frithelstock	Tavistock, St Eustace
Broadclyst	Ilfracombe, Holy Trinity	Thurlestone
Broadhembury	Ipplepen	Tiverton, St Peter
Cheriton Bishop	Little Hempston	Torbryan
Colyton	Milton Damerel	Totnes
Crediton	Ottery St Mary	

BIBLIOGRAPHY

Barber, Jennifer	'A Jigsaw in Stained Glass', *The Western Morning News*	
		18 September 1966
Boggis, R. J. E.	*A History of the Parish and Church of St Mary Magdalene,*	
	Barnstaple	1915
Boggis, R. J. E.	*A History of the Diocese of Exeter*	1922
Boggis, R. J. E.	*History of St John's, Torquay*	1930
Bond, Francis	*Fonts and Font Covers*	1908
Bond, F. B. and Camm, B.	*Roodscreens and Roodlofts*, Vol 2	1909
Bonham Carter, V.	*Exploring Parish Churches*	1961
Butters, F. C.	*Branscombe : The Parish and the Church*	1950
Cave, D.C.A. and Blakiston, C. H.	*A Short History of Sidbury Church*	1930
Chalk, E. S.	*History of St Peter's Church, Tiverton*	1905
Chanter, J. F.	*The Church of St James, Swimbridge*	n.d.
Chope, R. P.	*The Book of Hartland*	1940
Clark, Kenneth	*The Gothic Revival*	1950
Clarke, Basil F. L.	*Church Builders of the Nineteenth Century*	1938
Cook, G. H.	*The English Medieval Parish Church*	1954
Cooke, R. D.	*Notes on the Churches and Parishes of Ipplepen and Torbryan*	
	(3rd Edition)	1941
Coope, F. E.	*Thurlestone Church and Parish* (2nd Edition)	n.d.
Cornelius, C. Fryer	'Ancient Churches in the Deanery of Tavistock',	
	Archaeological Journal, Vol 15	1952
Cornelius, C. Fryer	*A Guide to St Andrew's Parish Church, Ashburton*	1960
Cox, J. Charles	'The Church of Branscombe', *The Reliquary*	January 1909
Cox, J. Charles	*Bench Ends in English Churches*	1916
Cresswell, Beatrix F.	*Exeter Churches*	1908
Cresswell, Beatrix F.	*Churches of the Deanery of Kenn*	1912
Cresswell, Beatrix F.	*The Collegiate Church of the Holy Cross, Crediton*	1922
Dalton, J. N.	*The Collegiate Church of Ottery St Mary*	1917
Davidson, James	*History of Axminster Church*	1835
Delderfield, Eric R.	*Church Furniture*	1967
Devon and Cornwall.	*Notes and Queries*	various
Devonshire Association,	*Transactions of the*	various
Drake, F. Morris	'The Painted Glass of Exeter Cathedral and other Devon	
	Churches', *Archaeological Journal*	1913
Drake, H. M.	*The Parish Church of Paignton*	1931
Duxbury, G. O. C.	*Bovey Tracey Parish Church*	1960
Esdaile, K. A.	*English Church Monuments* (1510-1840)	1946
Exeter Diocesan Architectural Society, Transactions of the		various
Exeter Diocesan Gazette	*Plymtree in Devon. Its Parish Church, Roodscreen,*	
	Manor and Rectors (reprinted as booklet 1956)	1905
Finberg, H. P. R.	*Tavistock Parish Church* (new edition)	1951
Giles, A. Linzie	*The Parish Church of St John Baptist, Paignton*	1911
Gill, Crispin	*Plymouth : A New History*	1966
Gray, Christopher	'The Screens of Devon', *Venture*	May 1965
Gurney, D. F.	*St James the Less, Plymouth*	1911
Hammond, Peter (edited by)	*Towards a Church Architecture*	1962
Hemms, Harry	'Roods and other screens in Devonshire Churches',	
	Journal of the Society of Architects, Vol 3	1896

Henderson, Charles	*The Cornish Church Guide and Parochial History of Cornwall*	1925
Hope, V.	*The Church and Parish of St Andrew, Colebrooke*	1952
Hoskins, W. G.	*Devon*	1954
Hoskins, W. G.	*Old Devon*	1966
Hughes, T. Cann	'Sir Stephen Glynn's Notes on the Churches of Devon'	
	Notes and Queries	1932
Hussell, Allen T.	*North Devon Churches*	1909
James, S. A. H.	*The Life Continues* (Charles and St Mathias Churches,	
	Plymouth)	1964
Jewitt, Llewellyn	*A History of Plymouth*	1873
King, A. Steele	*Branscombe, Its Church and Parish*	1923
King, Richard John	*The Church of St Mary and the Holy Cross at Crediton*	1876
Le Grice, F. E.	*The Story of the Parish Church of St John Baptist, Paignton*	n.d.
Little, Bryan	*Exeter* (including also Ottery St Mary, Crediton, Tiverton,	
	Cullompton, Topsham and Exmouth)	1953
Lough, A. G.	*The Church of St Mary the Virgin, Hennock*	1961
Mather, G.	*History of the Parish Church of St Michael, Beer*	n.d.
Mee, Arthur	*Devon* (The King's England)	1938
Morris, Joseph E.	*The Parish and Priory Church of St Mary, Totnes*	n.d.
Nesbitt, F.	*Ilfracombe Parish Church* (3rd Edition)	1937
Newman, Thomas	*The History of Coryton*	1940
Norway, Arthur H.	*A Short History of Sidmouth Parish Church* (7th Edition)	1962
Oliver, George	*Ecclesiastical Antiquities in Devon*	1840
Owen, T. R.	*St Brannock's Church, Braunton*	1963
Pevsner, Nikolaus	*The Buildings of England—North Devon*	1952
Pevsner, Nikolaus	*The Buildings of England—South Devon*	1952
Pevsner, Nikolaus	*Mediaeval Carvings in Exeter Cathedral*	1953
Plymouth Institution,	*Transactions of the*	various
Polwhele, R.	*The History of Devonshire*	1797
Prideaux, Edith K.	*Branscombe Church Architecturally Considered*	1911
Prideaux, Edith K.	*Sutcombe Church and its Builders*	1913
Reynolds, Herbert	*The Ancient Diocese of Exeter*	1895
Rogers, W. H. H.	*The Ancient Sepulchral Effigies of Devon*	1877
Rogers, W. H. H.	*Memorials of the West*	1888
Rogers, W. H. H.	*West Country Stories and Sketches*	1895
Rouse, Anthony	*St John's Church, Torquay*	n.d.
Searle, W. G.	*Anglo-Saxon Bishops, Kings and Nobles*	1899
Shaw, C. C.	*A History of the Parish of Aveton Giffard*	1966
Spreat, W.	*Churches of Devon*	1842
Stabb, John	*Some Old Devon Churches* (3 Vols) 1908, 1911, 1916	
Stabb, John	*Devon Church Antiquities* (Vol 1—all published)	1909
Summers, Vivian	*Church of the Holy Cross, Crediton*	n.d.
Taverner, R. L.	*The History of All Saints' Church, Okehampton*	1961
Thompson, A. H.	*The Ground Plan of the English Parish Church*	1911
Thompson, A. H.	'Church Architecture in Devon', *Archaeological Journal*	1913
Thompson, A. H.	*The Historical Growth of the English Parish Church*	1929
Vallance, Aymer	*English Church Screens*	1936
Welsford, A. E.	*The Parish Church of St Peter, Tiverton*	n.d.
Whiffen, Marcus	*Stuart and Georgian Churches*	1948
Whitham, John A.	*The Church of St Mary of Ottery*	n.d.
Wickham, A. K.	*Churches of Somerset* (2nd Edition)	1965
Wilson, W. G.	*The Church and Parish of Colyton*	n.d.
Worth, R. N.	*History of the Town and Borough of Devonport*	1890
Worth, R. N.	*History of Plymouth*	1890
Wrey, F. and C.	*A Guide to Tawstock Church* (3rd Edition)	1938

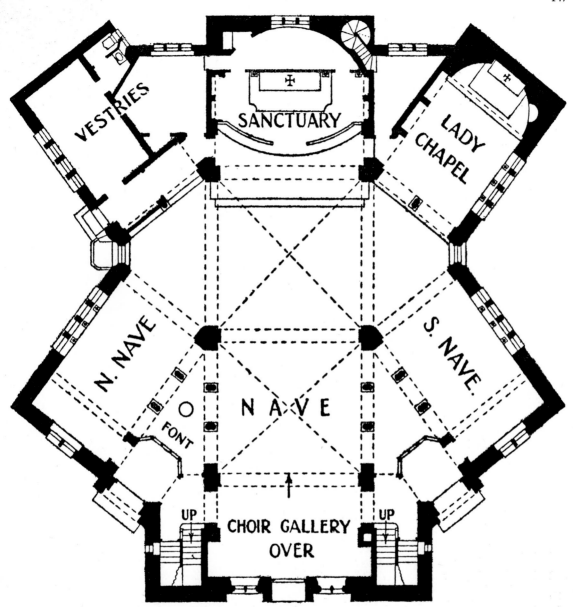

St Luke's Church, Milber, Newton Abbot.
The design of Milber is unique; it has been the subject of
worldwide interest and is among the finest churches built in these
islands during the present century. With three naves
radiating from the sanctuary, it is undoubtedly a new departure
in church planning (see photographs on pages 18 and 125)

TOPOGRAPHICAL REFERENCE

North *Devon*

1	Abbots Bickington	49	Clannaborough	97	Inwardleigh
2	Abbotsham	50	Clawton	98	Jacobstowe
3	Alverdiscott	51	Clayhanger	99	Kennerleigh
4	Alwington	52	Clovelly	100	Kentisbury
5	Appledore	53	Coldridge	101	Kings Nympton
6	Arlington	54	Combe Martin	102	Knowstone
7	Ashbury	55	Cookbury	103	Landcross
8	Ashford	56	Countisbury	104	Landkey
9	Ashreigney	57	Creacombe	105	Langtree
10	Ashwater	58	Cruwys Morchard	106	Lapford
11	Atherington	59	Dolton	107	Lifton
12	Bampton	60	Dowland	108	Littleham
13	Barnstaple	61	Down St Mary	109	Little Torrington
14	Beaford	62	East Anstey	110	Loxbeare
15	Beaworthy	63	East Buckland	111	Loxhore
16	Berrynarbor	64	East Down	112	Luffincott
17	Bideford	65	East Putford	113	Lundy
18	Bishops Nympton	66	East Worlington	114	Lynmouth
19	Bishops Tawton	67	Eggesford	115	Lynton
20	Bittadon	68	Exbourne	116	Mariansleigh
21	Black Torrington	69	Filleigh	117	Martinhoe
22	Bondleigh	70	Fremington	118	Marwood
23	Bow	71	Frithelstock	119	Meeth
24	Bradford	72	George Nympton	120	Merton
25	Bradworthy	73	Georgeham	121	Meshaw
26	Bratton Clovelly	74	Germansweek	122	Milton Damerel
27	Bratton Fleming	75	Goodleigh	123	Molland
28	Braunton	76	Great Torrington	124	Monkleigh
29	Brendon	77	Halberton	125	Monk Okehampton
30	Bridgerule	78	Halwill	126	Morchard Bishop
31	Broadwoodkelly	79	Hartland	127	Morebath
32	Broadwoodwidger	80	Hatherleigh	128	Mortehoe
33	Brushford	81	Heanton Punchardon	129	Newton St Petrock
34	Buckland Brewer	82	Highampton	130	Newton Tracey
35	Buckland Filleigh	83	High Bickington	131	Northam
36	Bulkworthy	84	Highbray	132	Northlew
37	Burlescombe	85	Hockworthy	133	North Molton
38	Burrington	86	Holcombe Rogus	134	North Tawton
39	Cadeleigh	87	Hollacombe	135	Nymet Rowland
40	Calverleigh	88	Holsworthy	136	Oakford
41	Challacombe	89	Honeychurch	137	Okehampton
42	Charles	90	Horwood	138	Pancrasweek
43	Chawleigh	91	Huish	139	Parkham
44	Cheldon	92	Huntsham	140	Parracombe
45	Cheriton Fitzpaine	93	Huntshaw	141	Petersmarland
46	Chittlehamholt	94	Iddesleigh	142	Petrockstow
47	Chittlehampton	95	Ilfracombe	143	Petton
48	Chulmleigh	96	Instow	144	Pilton

145 Poughill	201 Alphington	260 Clyst St Mary
146 Puddington	202 Ashburton	261 Cockington
147 Pyworthy	203 Ashcombe	262 Coffinswell
148 Rackenford	204 Ashprington	263 Cofton
149 Roborough	205 Ashton	264 Colaton Raleigh
150 Romansleigh	206 Aveton Giffard	265 Colebrooke
151 Rose Ash	207 Avonwick	266 Colyton
152 St Giles-in-the-Wood	208 Awliscombe	267 Combe-in-Teignhead
153 St Giles-on-the-Heath	209 Axminster	268 Combe Raleigh
154 Sampford Courtenay	210 Axmouth	269 Combpyne
155 Sampford Peverell	211 Aylesbeare	270 Cornwood
156 Satterleigh	212 Beer	271 Cornworthy
157 Shebbear	213 Belstone	272 Coryton
158 Sheepwash	214 Bere Alston	273 Cotleigh
159 Shirwell	215 Bere Ferrers	274 Crediton
160 South Molton	216 Berry Pomeroy	275 Crownhill
161 Stockleigh English	217 Bickington	276 Cullompton
162 Stoke Rivers	218 Bickleigh (Tiverton)	277 Culmstock
163 Stoodleigh	219 Bickleigh (Plymouth)	278 Dalwood
164 Stowford	220 Bicton	279 Dartington
165 Sutcombe	221 Bigbury	280 Dartmouth
166 Swimbridge	222 Bishopsteignton	281 Dawlish
167 Taddiport	223 Blackawton	282 Dean Prior
168 Tawstock	224 Blackborough	283 Denbury
169 Templeton	225 Bovey Tracey	284 Diptford
170 Tetcott	226 Bradninch	285 Dittisham
171 Thelbridge	227 Bradstone	286 Dodbrooke
172 Thornbury	228 Brampford Speke	287 Doddiscombsleigh
173 Thushelton	229 Branscombe	288 Drewsteignton
174 Trentishoe	230 Brentor	289 Dunchideock
175 Twitchen	231 Bridestowe	290 Dunkeswell
176 Uplowman	232 Bridford	291 Dunsford
177 Virginstowe	233 Brixham	292 Dunterton
178 Warkleigh	234 Brixton	293 East Allington
179 Washfield	235 Broadclyst	294 East Budleigh
180 Washford Pyne	236 Broadhembury	295 East Ogwell
181 Weare Giffard	237 Broadhempston	296 East Portlemouth
182 Welcombe	238 Buckerell	297 Egg Buckland
183 Wembworthy	239 Buckfast	298 Ermington
184 West Anstey	240 Buckfastleigh	299 Exeter
185 West Buckland	241 Buckland-in-the-Moor	300 Exminster
186 West Down	242 Buckland Monachorum	301 Exmouth
187 Westleigh	243 Budleigh Salterton	302 Farrington
188 West Putford	244 Butterleigh	302 Farringdon
189 Westward Ho!	245 Cadbury	304 Feniton
190 West Worlington	246 Chagford	305 Gidleigh
191 Winkleigh	247 Chardstock	306 Gittisham
192 Witheridge	248 Cheriton Bishop	307 Haccombe
193 Withleigh	249 Chivelstone	308 Halwell
194 Woolacombe	250 Christow	309 Harberton
195 Woolfardisworthy	251 Charleton	310 Harbertonford
196 Woolsery	252 Chudleigh	311 Harford
197 Yarnscombe	253 Churchstow	312 Harpford
198 Zeal Monachorum	254 Churston Ferrers	313 Hawkchurch
	255 Clayhidon	314 Hemyock
South Devon	256 Clyst Hidon	315 Hennock
	257 Clyst Honiton	316 Highweek
199 Abbotskerswell	258 Clyst St George	317 Hittisleigh
200 Alfington	259 Clyst St Lawrence	318 Holbeton

319	Holcombe Burnell	371	Northleigh	420	Staverton
320	Holne	372	Offwell	421	Stockland
321	Honiton	373	Otterton	422	Stockleigh Pomeroy
322	Horrabridge	374	Ottery St Mary	423	Stoke Canon
323	Huxham	375	Paignton	424	Stoke Fleming
324	Ide	376	Payhembury	425	Stoke Gabriel
325	Ideford	377	Peter Tavy	426	Stoke-in-Teignhead
326	Ilsington	378	Pinhoe	427	Stokenham
327	Ipplepen	379	Plymouth	428	Strete
328	Ivybridge		(including Devonport	429	Sydenham Damerel
329	Kelly		and Stonehouse)	430	Talaton
330	Kenn	380	Plympton	431	Tamerton Foliot
331	Kentisbeare	381	Plymstock	432	Tavistock
332	Kenton	382	Plymtree	433	Tedburn St Mary
333	Kilmington	383	Poltimore	434	Teigngrace
334	Kingsbridge	384	Powderham	435	Teignmouth
335	Kingskerswell	385	Princetown	436	Thorverton
336	Kingsteignton	386	Rattery	437	Throwleigh
337	Kingston	387	Rewe	438	Thurlestone
338	Kingswear	388	Ringmore	439	Tiverton
339	Lamerton	389	Rockbeare	440	Topsham
340	Landscove	390	Rousdon	441	Torbryan
341	Lewtrenchard	391	St John-in-the-Wilderness	442	Torquay
342	Littleham	392	Salcombe		(with Babbacombe)
343	Little Hempston	393	Salcombe Regis	443	Totnes
344	Loddiswell	394	Sandford	444	Trusham
345	Luppitt	395	Sampford Spiney	445	Uffculme
346	Lustleigh	396	Seaton	446	Ugborough
347	Lydford	397	Shaldon	447	Upexe
348	Lympstone	398	Shaugh Prior	448	Uplyme
349	Malborough	399	Sheldon	449	Upottery
350	Mamhead	400	Sheepstor	450	Upton Hellions
351	Manaton	401	Sherford	451	Upton Pyne
352	Maristow	402	Shillingford	452	Venn Ottery
353	Marldon	403	Shobrooke	453	Walkhampton
354	Marystow	404	Shute	454	Wembury
355	Mary Tavy	405	Sidbury	455	West Alvington
356	Meavy	406	Sidford	456	Westhill
357	Membury	407	Sidmouth	457	West Ogwell
358	Milton Abbot	408	Silverton	458	Whimple
359	Modbury	409	Slapton	459	Whitchurch
360	Monkton	410	Sourton	460	Whitestone
361	Moretonhampstead	411	South Brent	461	Widecombe-in-the-Moor
362	Morleigh	412	South Huish	462	Widworthy
363	Musbury	413	Southleigh	463	Willand
364	Netherexe	414	South Milton	464	Woodbury
365	Newton Abbot	415	South Pool	465	Woodland
366	Newton Ferrers	416	South Tawton	466	Woodleigh
367	Newton Poppleford	417	South Zeal	467	Yarcombe
368	Newton St Cyres	418	Sowton	468	Yealmpton
369	North Bovey	419	Spreyton	469	Yelverton
370	North Huish				

DEVON: topographical reference

GLOSSARY OF ARCHITECTURAL TERMS

ABACUS	flat slab on the top of a capital
ARABESQUE or GROTESQUE	light and fanciful surface decoration using combinations of flowing lines, tendrils, etc, interspersed with vases, animals, etc
ASHLAR	masonry of large block wrought to even faces and square edges
BATTER	wall with an inclined face
BATTLEMENT	parapet with a series of indentations
BEAKHEAD	Norman ornamental motif consisting of a row of bird or beast heads with beaks
BILLET	Norman ornamental motif made up of short raised rectangles placed at regular intervals
BLOCK or CUSHION CAPITAL	Romanesque capital cut from a cube by having the lower angles rounded off to the circular shaft below
BOSS	knob or projection usually placed to cover the intersection of ribs in a vault
CAPITAL	head or top part of a column
CASTELLATED	decorated with battlements
CELURE	adorned part of wagon roof above rood or altar
CHAMFER	surface made by cutting across the square angle of a stone block, etc, at an angle of 45° to the two other surfaces
CHEVRON	sculptured moulding forming a zig-zag
CLERESTORY	upper storey of the nave walls pierced by windows
CORBEL	block of stone projecting from a wall, supporting some horizontal feature
CREST, CRESTING	ornamental finish along the top of a screen
CROCKET, CROCKETING	decorative features placed on the sloping sides of spires, pinnacles, gables, etc
CUPOLA or LANTERN	small polygonal or circular domed turret crowning a roof
CUSP	in tracery the small pointed member between two lobes of a trefoil, quatrefoil, etc
DADO	decorative covering of the lower part of a wall
EASTER SEPULCHRE	recess with tomb-chest usually in the wall of a chancel, the tomb-chest to receive an effigy of Christ for Easter celebrations
FILLET	narrow flat band running down a shaft or along a roll moulding
FINIAL	the top of a pinnacle, gable or bench-end carved into a leaf or leaf-like form
FOIL	lobe formed by the cusping of a circle or an arch. Trefoil, quatrefoil, cinquefoil express the number of leaf shapes to be seen
FOLIATED	carved with leaf shapes
GARGOYLE	water spout carved into a human or animal shape
JAMB	straight side of an archway, doorway or window
LINENFOLD	Tudor panelling ornamented with a conventional representation of a piece of linen laid in vertical folds

MISERICORD	bracket placed on the underside of the seat of a choir-stall, to afford rest to a person standing
PARVISE	room over a church porch
PEDIMENT	low-pitched gable used in Classical, Renaissance and neo-Classical architecture above doors, windows, etc
PENDANT	boss elongated so that it seems to hang down
PILASTER	shallow pier attached to a wall
PISCINA	basin for washing the Communion or Mass vessels, provided with a drain
PLINTH	projecting base of a wall or column
QUOINS	dressed stones at the angles of a building
REREDOS	structure behind and above an altar
RESPOND	half-pier bounded into a wall and carrying one end of an arch
RUBBLE	building stones, not square or hewn, nor laid in regular courses
SALTIRE CROSS	equal-limbed cross placed diagonally
SCALLOPED CAPITAL	development of the block capital in which the single semi-circular surface is elaborated into a series of truncated cones
SEDILIA	seats for the priests (usually three) on the south side of the chancel
SILL	lower horizontal part of the frame of a window
SOFFIT	undersurface of an arch
SPANDREL	the space between the shoulder of an arch and the rectangular moulding, etc, enclosing it, or between the shoulders of adjoining arches and the moulding, etc
SPLAY	chamfer, usually of a jamb of a window
SPRINGING	level at which an arch rises from its supports
STRAPWORK	sixteenth-century decoration consisting of interlaced bands
TABERNACLE	richly ornamented niche or free-standing canopy
TRANSOME	horizontal bar across the opening of a window
VOUSSOIR	wedge-shaped stone used in arch construction
WAINSCOT	timber lining to walls

INDEX—PLACE NAMES

Illustrations are indicated by page references in **bold** type

INDEX—PERSONAL NAMES